Bequeathed to the
Colorado Arts & Crafts Society
by friend and cofounder
Nancy Strathearn

Haddonfield
Historic Homes

Haddonfield Historic Homes
Success Through Historic Preservation

Written and edited by Joan L. Aiken
Photographs by Jim Cooper

A Publication of the Haddonfield Preservation Society

HARROWOOD BOOKS / PUBLISHERS

First published in the United States of America in 1991 by Harrowood Books
3943 N. Providence Rd., Newtown Square, PA 19073

Library of Congress Cataloging-in-Publication Data

Aiken, Joan L.
    Haddonfield historic homes: success through historic preservation
    edited by Joan L. Aiken; photographs by Jim Cooper.
    p.   cm.
    "A publication of the Haddonfield Preservation Society."
    ISBN 0-915180-33-2: $55.00
    1. Historic buildings—New Jersey—Haddonfield. 2. Dwellings—New Jersey—Haddonfield.
 3. Architecture, Domestic—New Jersey—Haddonfield. 4. Haddonfield (N.J.)—Buildings, structures, etc.
5. Dwellings—New Jersey—Haddonfield—Pictorial works. 6. Haddonfield (N.J.)—Description—Views.
I. Haddonfield Preservation Society.   II. Title.
F144.H15A35 1991
974.9'87—dc20   91-18808
                                                                      CIP

DESIGN BY PAUL NIGEL HARRIS AND JAMES A. BOYLE
SET IN TYPE BY MICHAEL TYPOGRAPHY, MEDIA, PENNSYLVANIA
PRINTED AND BOUND IN KOREA

To Henry D. M. Sherrerd
whose vision and support opened the door
to historic preservation in Haddonfield

SPONSORS

*Special acknowledgments and
appreciation to these
sponsors of "Haddonfield Historic
Homes," whose generous support made
this publication possible*

James G. Aiken, Esq.
Archer & Greiner
   A Professional Corporation
Henry D. Bean
The Borda Family
Joan and William Brown
William Carroll
Dr. and Mrs. Donald E. Clark
Donald C. Cofsky, Esq.
Commissioner Letitia
   and Dr. Daniel Colombi
Covenant Bank
Arthur and Janet Craig
Mr. and Mrs. W. Robert Davis
DeLong, Born, Iannacone, Dalsey
   Orthopaedic Surgery
E. Guy Elzey, Jr.
E. Guy Elzey, III
William Parker Freeman
Carol and Philip Fuoco
John J. and Christine Gallagher, Jr.
William J. Gallo, AIA
Robert Gaunt Company
Debra and Mario Gebbia
Samuel Gerstein, Esq.
   and Diane B. Cohen, Esq.
Louis H. Goettelmann, AIA
Mrs. Elmer L. Grimes
The Haddon Fortnightly
Haddonfield Garden Club

Mrs. Thelma R. Hall
Joseph F. Haro
Robert W. Hill, AIA and Eleanor D. Hill
Richard M. Hluchan, Esq.
Mr. and Mrs. Joseph S. Holman
Houshiarnejad Collection
Emily and Howard Johnson
Myra and Gene Kain
Robert C. Kay Family
Mr. and Mrs. Saverio Lacroce
Lawrence and Bonnie Legnola
Mark and Christine Lenny
Dr. and Mrs. Courtney M. Malcarney
Anthony Minyon
Horace G. Moeller
Johan Gordon Nilsen, AIA
Ralph Pendrak, AIA
Plastics & Resins, Inc.
Presbyterian Home in Haddonfield
Remington & Vernick, Engineers
James C. Rhoads
The Riggs Family
Roney, Vermaat & Leonard, Realtors
Mayor Jack and Barbara Tarditi
James C. Tassini, MD
Mr. and Mrs. William. H. Taylor
Mr. and Mrs. Robert J. Twitchell
Charles J. Weiler, AIA
Rosalind Williams
Williamson Design, Architects

CONTENTS

Acknowledgments

Greatest thanks are due to the many who contributed their assistance to the realization of this book. The scholarly research on the history of the historic homes is the work of Elizabeth Hopkins Lenhart, Mary Jane Freedley, Caroline B. Moody, Lee Albright, William J. Blake, Myra Kain, and Henry Watson, Jr. We were most fortunate to have leading local architects provide the architectural descriptions of the houses – Louis H. Goettelmann, William Brookover, Charles J. Weiler, Ralph Pendrak, Don Stevenson, and William J. Gallo, former chairman of the Historic Preservation Commission, now located in Florida, who in addition to the excellent descriptions came up to Haddonfield frequently to lend his creative talent to the production of the book. Our special thanks to Katherine Tassini, librarian of the Haddonfield Historical Society, and Douglas Rauschenberger, director of the Public Library, who were extremely helpful in our research efforts, and to Pat Lennon for her fine account of the early architects and builders. We were also fortunate to have the assistance of Camden County historian William Leap, who generously gave his considerable knowledge to the account of the early history of Haddonfield. A delightful and rewarding part of our task were the personal interviews with many of the owners of the historic homes from whom we gleaned the feeling and association that enlivens history. We are most grateful to the Co-Chairmen of the Finance Committee, Horace G. Moeller, William H. Taylor, and Mayor John J. Tarditi, Jr., whose fund-raising efforts made the production of the book possible. Our appreciation also to Dr. Roger W. Moss, author and lecturer, for permission to reprint the excellent glossary from his book, "Victorian Exterior Decoration." And to our Publisher, Paul Harris of Harrowood Books, for his patient and expert guidance through the complexities of publishing and the exceptional artistry of the production. We also owe a debt of gratitude to Dr. Charles Lee, a staunch and long-time friend, who urged us for many years to undertake the project and found for us an excellent publisher.

HADDONFIELD HISTORIC HOMES

is also a tribute to the late Elizabeth Hopkins Lenhart
who passed away unexpectedly on May 2, 1990, and who, as
official historian of the Preservation Society, left a legacy of
research and writings on Haddonfield historic homes, a
principal resource for this book.

Our Architectural Heritage

by Joan L. Aiken

Haddonfield's rich heritage is not locked in a museum; it is displayed in historic buildings.

How will we know it's us without our past.

—John Steinbeck

In the libraries, on shelves end to end, are books that deal one way or another with the early homes of New Jersey, including those in Haddonfield. Indeed it would seem from the dozen titles on my own bookshelf that the subject of our heritage houses had by now been pretty well explored. Not until now has any book portrayed the historic homes of Haddonfield as they really are in color, with their cultural histories and architectural descriptions. How many people who pass these houses every day have ever been aware of what beauties are to be encountered, what choice architectural features to look for?

Through "HADDONFIELD HISTORIC HOMES," the public can become acquainted with the most historically significant and endearing of all the town's natural resources. We have selected for this book houses which have been preserved and restored, not demolished or lost to decay, so that anyone can walk through the town today and see our visual history. Homes in this book are in the Historic District, established in 1971, or will be soon with the planned extension of the District. They are arranged in the sequence of a "walking tour," so you can grasp, not only the house, but how and when the street developed. We have chosen houses and buildings representative of each street in the Historic District, good examples of a distinctive period style, omitting houses which have been so altered that their original architectural integrity has been obliterated.

The streets in the Historic District are those in the old historic core of the town. "King's Road," now King's Highway, was laid out in 1681 over a portion of the trail of the Lenni Lenape Indians, running from Perth Amboy to Salem. The road completed in 1686 was constructed 100 feet wide for the King of England and his entourage to visit his colony. It was a one street town which developed along this main artery, and then, as the town grew, down side streets leading off King's Highway. The boundaries of the Historic District were thus established.

The selection of houses in this book exemplifies the architectural development of the town, from the first permanent structures of the early colonial settlement, through the Federal period of the young nation and the diversity of 19th century styles. The selection includes houses of the great and of the not so great, of the wealthy who built extensive and luxurious houses and those in modest circumstances, even the simple tradesman, who gave a highly picturesque effect to his humble home. In all cases, they are significant expressions of Haddonfield's experience and tradition. Each speaks reliably of a particular place and time in history, and of certain social and individual circumstances. They all speak of the needs and dreams and tastes of the people who owned and lived in them, homes of men and women who literally have left their mark on the land. In a number of cases, the interest and importance of these homes is magnified by association with the lives of men and women who have played some memorable part in the community's past.

ORIGINS

Three main factors determined the architecture of New Jersey and of Haddonfield. One, the heritage of the people who settled here. Two, the reflection of the racial, political, economic and religious sequence of the colony, and then the state. Three, the availability of building material. New Jersey was settled by peoples from many lands who contributed elements of their heritage to the first architecture of the settlement. This inheritance from the old country and the nature of available materials governed the character of the early buildings. Land was the basis of the development of settlements and its material resources and productivity gave diversity to its architecture.

In Haddonfield we see the restrictive influence of the religious Quakers, our first settlers, upon early architectural exuberance. The lack of ostentation or ornament on either exteriors or interiors prior to the first quarter of the 19th century is undoubtedly the result of religious teaching as much as inheritance. We see early buildings undertaken with a general scheme of balance but the lack of plans and drawings, and the crudeness of tools led to errors in calculation and compromises of structural difficulties which resulted in those rugged irregularities that mark early work with an especial and delightful individuality.

As for building materials, in forested South Jersey, wood is the preponderant building material. Brick, a mark of elegance, was either brought from England or made on the premises by craftsmen who had learned their trade in England. We know there was a brickyard in Haddonfield, and that Francis Collins, the earliest settler in 1682, built his home "Mountwell," partly of brick, as he had

In this country, instead of palaces, temples, tombs or cathedrals, the real historical monuments are the fine old homes that tell the history of our American people. They keep a personal and appealing record of the way people lived when the nation was young.

Early American Homes,
Richard Pratt

apprenticed as a bricklayer in London before emigrating to America. And in 1713, Elizabeth Haddon Estaugh built her first house in what is now Haddonfield of brick and wood. Brick is the material of the 1732 Guard Houses, the 1750 Indian King Tavern and the 1758 Shivers-French-Tatem house, and many of our Federal period houses.

THE LANDOWNERS

The buying and selling of real estate was big business in the early settlement as it is today. It was a principal means of income. John Haddon, father of Elizabeth Haddon, owned vast holdings in this region, though he never left England for the new country. Owners of the largest tracts were John Gill, the John Kay family, the Collins family and the Thomas Redmans. These early settlers not only owned and sold parcels of land, they and their descendents built impressive homes on their land, reflecting their prosperity. Through her father, Elizabeth Haddon and her husband John Estaugh acquired considerable land and property, extending from Cooper's Creek along the line of Maple Avenue to Newton Creek to near Avondale Avenue, thence to the King's Highway to Cooper's Creek, including land sold to John Gill, her cousin. Her land holdings, more or less, determined the street plan of the village.

In the late summer of 1713, John Haddon wrote to Elizabeth and John, addressing them as "Most Dear Children," and telling them that as he had invested so heavily in America he wanted them to sell as much land as necessary to get such things as they wanted, the house and orchard and whatever you desire is yours and we hope you will be made comfortable."

THE DEVELOPERS

As Haddonfield entered the decade of the 1850's the anticipation of the development of the Camden and Atlantic Railroad, in 1852, promoted by a few Haddonfield businessmen, the first railroad to be built completely across the state to the Atlantic Ocean, bringing vast areas of southern New Jersey into productive use, gave rise to several real estate development companies. With building plans and extravagant promotional literature they fully expected a

building boom which never materialized, as their ambitious projects failed.

The Haddonfield Land and Improvement Company entertained the hope of building up the town on the 130 acres of the old Mountwell tract. In the 1850's the Ready Villa Association came forth with a planned suburban development at the eastern end of the town, with a proposal for a second railroad. The purpose of the Association was to pool the funds of the middle class families in order to build a self-contained community of country homes and summer cottages within a park-like setting. The homes were to be designed by no less an architect than the popular Samuel Sloan of Philadelphia who planned three sizes of double cottages and laid out the plan for the community. Despite an elaborate prospectus, the real estate schemes failed. No reasons are given in any of the existing accounts for the failure of these projects, but the panic of 1857, which brought an end to the real estate boom throughout the area, may have affected both plans. Another factor may have been the conservatism and general lack of enthusiasm among the native Haddonfield residents for growth which they felt would raise their taxes and change the character of their quiet country village. Samuel Sloan's entire landscape plan has survived and a copy is in the Philadelphia Public Library and in the Haddonfield Historical Society. It is believed that the plans for one of these double cottages were copied by a builder and were used to construct the double house at 40-42 Warwick Road, which indeed follows the Sloan plan.

STYLES

Through Jim Cooper's photographs and their architectural descriptions, we get a powerful sense of the visual history of Haddonfield, the architectural styles that evolved over the eighteenth and nineteenth centuries, and into the dawn of the twentieth century. Seen in its totality, we can view Haddonfield, not as a restored colonial town, frozen in time, but as a place where natural environment, artistic tradition, and historic context, produced what has been acknowledged from its early village days to the present as a "beautiful town," continuing to resist, as with the Ready Villa and other early development plans, the pressures to change its "country village" character.

Here is a microcosm of early domestic architecture in America. In this town are examples of the principal development of architectural styles through the Colonial, Federal and Victorian periods. In "HADDONFIELD HISTORIC HOMES" you will find these examples—Simple Colonial, Later Georgian Colonial, Federal, Greek Revival, Gothic Revival, Carpenter Gothic, Italianate, Second Empire, Stick Style, Queen Anne and Colonial Revival.

Most important, throughout Haddonfield, as throughout the nation, our architectural heritage gives that uniqueness and distinction, those delightful physical characteristics of an age noted for its individual expression, not mass volume, for local variants of the great design masters, whether simple or elegant, when every carpenter, builder, hardware maker was a master craftsman...when there was not the mobility of the automobile and uprooting moves...and a house was built for forever, to be lived in and loved by generation after generation.

Village of pleasant lanes,
Village of tree tops where wild birds come,
Village of welcoming church spires,
Village of cheering hearth-fires,
Village where the neighbor spirit reigns,
Village of Children – Home!

— James Lane Pennypacker, 1913
Verse and Prose
(published 1936, Historical Society of Haddonfield)

"Birdwood," 1794

William Estaugh Hopkins House
Hopkins Lane

Here may be found these relics of by-gone days that have escaped the too often vandal hand of progress.
Hon. John Clement, Haddonfield, 1877

This lovely, colonial-style country house in its original sylvan setting, surrounded by centuries old white, black, red and Spanish Oaks and a wondrous allée of beech trees, is the ancestral home of the most illustrious family in Haddonfield history-five generations of Hopkins.

In its modern history it has been the home of the Driscoll family, Birdwood having been purchased in 1933 by the late Alfred E. Driscoll, elected Governor of New Jersey in 1946. During its almost 200-year history, the house has seen architectural changes, additions, alterations and restorations, reflecting the changing needs, tastes and fortunes of its owners. It began as a four-room house, two rooms and a hall downstairs; two bedrooms and a hall upstairs, a small room and attic space above, built by John Estaugh Hopkins in 1794 for his son William upon his marriage to Ann Morgan, great, great granddaughter of Griffeth Morgan, whose house built in 1693, now restored as a museum, still stands on the bank of the Delaware River in Pennsauken, N.J. It was Ann Morgan who named the estate "Birdwood" capturing in its name the deep woods and vivid bird life she dearly loved.

The house had its historic origins in the land upon which it stands, belonging to Francis Collins, Haddonfield's first white settler in 1682, who wanted access to a landing on the Cooper River. In 1746, for the supposed purpose of lumbering, Ebenezer Hopkins, grandnephew and heir of Elizabeth Haddon Estaugh, credited with founding the village of Haddonfield, purchased from a grandson of Francis Collins this tract of 117 acres of woodland. We are indebted to him for leaving many of the best trees which have survived today. Upon the death of Ebenezer in 1757 the property passed to his son, John Estaugh Hopkins who, thirty years later, in 1789, built a grist mill on the property naming it Haddon Mill. The builder was Major William Ellis, a Revolutionary War veteran, who used Pennsylvania stone shipped by flat boat up Cooper's Creek to Stoys Landing.

When John's son William came of age in 1794, having shown great interest in the mill, his father turned its management over to him, and the same year built the first house on the tract for his son.

The first major alteration of Birdwood was in 1845 when a two-story addition was erected to accommodate the Hopkins seven children. The demarcation of the old part and later addition is easily seen in a seam between the two parts, and in the siding and windows. The old part has the fine detail of beaded siding, not repeated in the later addition. In the original part first floor windows have 12 over 12 panes; second floor windows, 12 over 8 panes, an early colonial characteristic. Windows in the new part are 6 over 6 panes. The original 6-panel Dutch door remains with a charming sidelight window on the right, as do all the 3-panel shutters; also the elegant 1845 Palladian window on the side gable. The Hopkins all left widows who fell on hard times and were forced to sell bits and pieces of the land, even original interior paneling, fireplace mantels - there was one in every room - and the beautiful handmade hardware. The century old boxwood was sold to Winterthur but subsequently replaced in the 20th century. For a while the house was run as a tavern; the front family room is still called the "tap room." In the late 19th century, the vogue of Victorian architecture overtook Birdwood and old photos show a Victorian, bracketed porch across the old part of the house and brackets under the roof. Later, an inappropriate boxlike glass enclosed sun room was added. But to the last Hopkins resident, despite hard times, this distinguished family was able to save the family home. It was Alfred Driscoll and his wife Antoinette, with their scholarly interest in colonial architecture, who made the significant changes we see today with its colonial character reflecting their frequent visits to Williamsburg and their attendance in the early years of their marriage at the symposiums on colonial architecture. The offending Victorian porch and sun room were removed. With the professional guidance of local architect Ellery Taylor, a third floor office-bedroom was added to the two-story 1845 addition with colonial dormer windows and a wood shingle roof to match the original roof. The windows were designed to catch the view of the deep woods, beloved of all Birdwood owners and residents. Later, a modern kitchen wing was added retaining part of the stone wall of the old mill.

Above: *Fireplace mantel in "Birdwood" living room is made of King of Prussia Blue Marble, in a Classic Revival design, probably erected when the house was enlarged in 1854. Eighteenth century fireplace was sold. Corner cupboard and andirons are original, from the 1794 Hopkins house and never left "Birdwood."*

Above: *Paneled wall in dining room of "Birdwood" was constructed during Governor Driscoll's residence. The design was influenced by Williamsburg architecture in which the Driscolls had a scholarly interest.*

Isaac H. Wood House, 1842

201 Wood Lane

Hail to the fathers of our ancient town!
They little thought their deeds would bring renown,
They wished to benefit and with this view,
They wisely built, and better than they knew.
　　　　　　John E. Redman, Haddonfield, 1905

This elegant example of the Greek Revival style in a Haddonfield residence was built by Isaac Wood, the patriarch of a distinguished farming family. No house in this town is more closely associated with Elizabeth Haddon, the founder of the village, as here stood the first home she and her husband John Estaugh built in 1713, which was tragically destroyed by fire on April 14, 1842. Situated on the highest point of the 500 acre tract, the original brick mansion and plantation were willed, upon the death of the widowed and childless Elizabeth Estaugh in 1762 to her nephew's children, the Ebenezer Hopkins family.

The estate, named "New Haddonfield" fell in disrepair and passed in and out of the Hopkins family until 1829 when Elizabeth H. Cooper, of the noted Camden Cooper family, bought the house and 150 acres of the farm at a sheriff's sale for $6,200. Two years later she married Isaac Wood, a flourishing farmer. The couple had one daughter and six sons. Their portraits, handsome gentry, hang in the parlors of Greenfield Hall, now the headquarters of the Historical Society.

During that fateful night of April 14, the disastrous fire started in the kitchen. The Wood family escaped and with the help of friends and neighbors were able to save much of the beautiful furniture which Elizabeth had brought back from England. The house and kitchen were entirely destroyed but the barns and outbuildings escaped fire. Still standing is the 1713 brick "Brew House." The boxwood trees planted by Elizabeth from cuttings she brought from her native country a hundred years before were saved from damage when Isaac Wood covered them with wet carpets. By 1910 the tallest boxwood had grown to 25 feet and its trunk was 17 inches in diameter. Her yew tree, now a towering giant, is seen at the right foreground of the Wood home. As soon as the bricks had cooled from the fire, work began on the new home. The original foundation of Pennsylvania stone was repaired by John A. Swinker, a noted builder of the time. The old bricks were cleaned by twenty-six men and two boys within two weeks of the fire. It was necessary to buy 31,500 new bricks.

While farming operations continued, local craftsmen and builders set to work to build the new house which is said to have been completed on October 5, 1842, a little more than six months after the fire. Isaac Wood died at the farm in 1879, his wife Elizabeth, the following year. The property passed to his fourth son, Samuel Wood who, for 65 years, was a leader in the community life of Haddonfield, and held important posts in business and government in the Delaware Valley. He was president of the Haddonfield National Bank and a member of the Executive Committee of the Farmer's Association, organized to take important actions to relieve the farmers of impositions practiced upon them. He was killed in April, 1929, when his horse and buggy was hit by a bus.

In 1943, the house was purchased by Frederick Fox, Jr., a local realtor who became a Commissioner of Haddonfield, and later subdivided the property to build a row of single homes facing Merion Avenue. He saved the mellow old bricks from the original fence which was removed, and used them to build the brick front of his office at 70 Tanner Street.

Notable and typical architectural features of this Greek Revival style house are the front portico with its four classic Doric fluted columns, the simple entablature above, the small attic story windows in the frieze. The four-paneled shutters, the paneled double doors and rectangular transom are features of the period. The portico balustrade was found in the cellar in good shape by the present owners who repaired and replaced it. The charming original carriage entrance on the left of the building with its graceful details was also repaired. The pared-down simplicity of this home is typical of the Greek Revival aesthetic and achieved national popularity in residential and non-residential designs. Every beautiful detail of this great house, the only one of its kind in Haddonfield, is now preserved under the Historic District Ordinance.

Above: *Elizabeth Haddon Estaugh Brew House, 1713, 201 Wood Lane, the oldest building still standing in Haddonfield. This brick building, at the rear of the Isaac Wood mansion, was the only part of the original Elizabeth Estaugh 1713 home and accessory buildings which was not destroyed by fire in 1841. This charming building, originally one-story, was used by the young founder of the village of Haddonfield to prepare medicines from herbs and plants with which she tended the inhabitants of the small settlement, and her friends, the Indians. It is said that the Brew House was used to brew beer, a common enterprise among the early settlers. A four-foot fireplace is at one side of the middle of the building, the remains of the still on its right, and its pewter draincock for drawing off the completed liquid, is still intact.*

"This Pleasant Town"
Early History

This is a very pleasant town, built upon both sides of a wide road along which extends for more than a half a mile. The houses are of brick and wood, many of them neat and commodious and surrounded by gardens, orchard and grass lots.

Thomas S. Gordon, publisher
Gordon's Gazetteer - 1834

More than fifty years later, in 1889, Haddonfield was still acclaimed "a pleasant town." John Van Court, Editor of "The Basket," the town's first newspaper, wrote:

Among the many beautiful towns and villages that dot the landscape for miles around Philadelphia, Haddonfield, in all those desirable features that go to make up an ideal suburban home, stands pre-eminent.

And in an account of Haddonfield in a book published in 1882 on *The Industries of New Jersey,* there appears the recognition:

One of the most inviting towns in Camden County is Haddonfield which is located on the line of the Camden and Atlantic Railroad, six miles from Philadelphia and fifty-five from Atlantic City. It is one of the cleanest and best kept towns within a short distance of Philadelphia, and is a popular place of residence for many of the business men of the latter city during the summer months.

What were the forces that created "this pleasant town?" First and foremost, the character of the people who settled here; secondly, its advantageous location, and above all the strong determination of its citizens to maintain and preserve its basic values and tradition.

FIRST SETTLERS

The first settlers were Quakers, persecuted for their religion in England, who sought not only religious freedom in the new country, but a better life and future for themselves and their children. They brought with them the moral values and simplicity of life style that had the most profound influence on the town through more than 300 years.

Among these first settlers, Francis Collins, born in Oxfordshire, England in 1635, stands out. On June 2, 1677, Collins purchased 4/7 of a Proprietary share in the colony of West New Jersey, giving him rights to land, not already taken, anywhere within the colony. This acquisition of land in the "New World" and his experiences as a victim of persecution as a Quaker prompted him to emigrate to America with his family. They arrived in Burlington, the provincial Capitol, between 1677 and 1680.

Although Collins had apprenticed as a bricklayer in England, during his brief stay in Burlington he apparently was engaged in farming, a necessary occupation in the wilderness of New Jersey at the time. The survey for his Haddonfield land identifies him as a "yeoman," (a farmer.) During his time in Burlington he also sought out the most desirable location for his homestead. He selected land on the west side of Cooper's Creek in which is now the entire southeastern part of Haddonfield. On October 23, 1682, this tract of 500 acres was surveyed to him as a portion of his proprietary holdings.

Undoubtedly at the time of the survey, Collins had already built his house and was residing on the site, as was the custom. The house was located on a hill facing a main Indian trail that was in the process of being blazed as the first "Great Roade" of the colony, by order on November 25, 1681, of the General Assembly. It became known as the "Burlington-Salem Roade." Collins named his plantation "Mountwell." His house stood near the intersection of today's Centre Street and Cottage Avenue. Subsequent acquisitions of land increased his holdings westward to the south branch of Newton Creek and northward into what is now Westmont, making him Haddonfield's largest land holder. He was also one of the most distinguished citizens of the new settlement, elected to represent the "third tenth" in the provincial assembly in 1683, reelected in 1684, and serving as one of the judges of the courts of what became Gloucester County. Before removing to Burlington in 1686 at the urging of his second wife, Mary Gosling, a native of the Capitol, he is remembered as the first European settler to have made a significant mark on "Haddonfield."

Mountwell remained in the Collins family through marriages until the late 1820's when it was purchased by John Gill IV, a direct descendent of Francis Collins. When Gill moved to his new mansion on King's Highway in 1841, it was sold to the Haddonfield Land and Improvement Company, whose plans for development of the property failed. Several owners later, Rev. T. Maxwell

ESTAUGH HOUSE.
1776 – LADIES' CENTENNIAL TEA PARTY, 1874. – 1876
HADDONFIELD, N.J.

Above: Elizabeth Haddon Estaugh House, 1713, drawing from an original painting by Thomas Redman, 1830's.

Reilly bought Mountwell in 1870 and moved his St. Johns Academy here from Burlington in 1871. About April 15, 1872, Mountwell was destroyed by fire.

Elizabeth Haddon, the most revered name in the history of Haddonfield, and a powerful influence in its development, is credited with the founding and naming of the village in 1713. Her romantic story, told in fact, fiction and poetry begins in England about six years after Francis Collins was established at Mountwell. A little girl of eight years, one of the two daughters of John Haddon, a well-educated and wealthy Quaker entrepreneur, was captivated by the visit of William Penn, a devoted friend of the Haddons. She listened spellbound as he described the American Indians, their beaded moccasins, colorful blankets, wigwams and strange culture. He talked of vast forests, sparkling streams and plentiful game and gave her an ear of Indian corn he had brought her. An Indian papoose doll became her dearest possession. Thus the seed was sown that blossomed in 1701 when Elizabeth, barely twenty-one years of age, prevailed upon her father to send her to America to take up the option on 500 acres of land on Cooper's Creek, which required that he take possession in six months. Circumstances prevented the Haddons from emigrating to the new world, but like many others who never came to America, he speculated in its real estate. He owned or had proprietary rights to thousands of acres from Salem County to above the Falls of the Delaware. And so he sent the adventurous, courageous Elizabeth with full power to transact business in his name.

She was met at the port of Philadelphia by William Penn, then crossed the Delaware by barge with her servants and possessions, where she was met at Cooper's Creek landing by members of the Collins family. Her first home was a log house which, through her gracious hospitality and good deeds, became a universal resort to Friends traveling to Newton meeting, the place of worship in the region for the Quakers. One of these was John Estaugh, a young Quaker minister, whom she married a year later. The Estaughs built their first home in what is now Haddonfield in 1713, a handsome brick mansion on land given to them by her father at the location, now 201 Wood Lane. She named it New Haddonfield after her father, John Haddon (Haddon Fields), thus giving this town its name.

The real "founding" of the village came later when, far more important, she and her father deeded in 1721 a piece of land on Haddon Avenue, near King's Highway to the Religious Society of Friends for a Meeting House and cemetery. The first meeting for worship was held on December 12, 1721. For the next 97 years, it was the only place of worship in Haddonfield. This brought the focus of people from old Newton Township Meeting House toward Haddonfield as a more convenient location for worship. Thus Elizabeth and John Estaugh established Haddonfield as the religious center of the area, an important factor in the growth of the village.

The romantic tale of the young English girl who sailed to the New World, "proposed" marriage to the young Quaker minister, John Estaugh, on their way to Meeting, established the village of Haddonfield, and left an indelible mark on the community, has been told in poems and stories. The most celebrated is the poem "Elizabeth," by Henry Wadsworth Longfellow, in the Theologian's Tale from "Tales of a Wayside Inn."

Well documented is that she became known as the outstanding woman of all time in old Gloucester County. She had become as proficient as her husband in the use of medicine, having learned many remedies from the Indians as well. Her kindnesses and charities were well

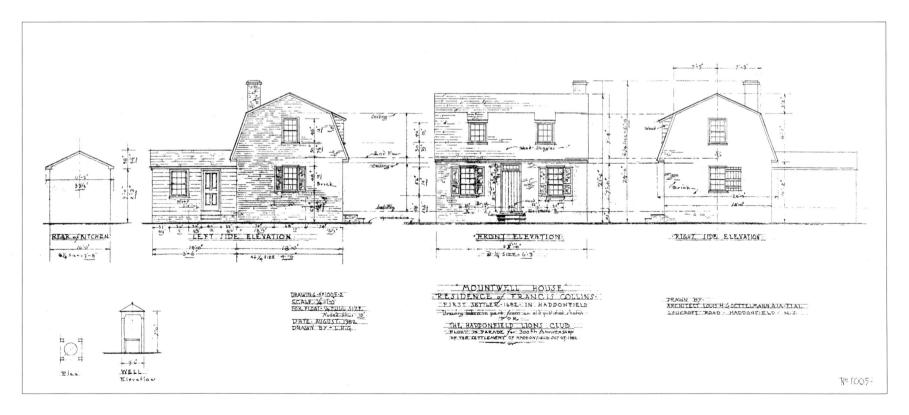

Above: *Mountwell House — Drawing of "Mountwell" by Louis H. Goettelmann, AIA, from an old sketch.*

known. That she was a woman of education and intellect is obvious from her letters and business dealings. Her cultivated taste and refinement was exhibited in the beautiful colonial design of the Estaugh house and the furniture brought over from England, several pieces of which have become collector's treasures, acquisitions of the Historical Society, and in private collections. Her husband, John Estaugh, died in 1742. Just before Elizabeth died in 1762 at the age of 82, Benjamin Franklin, the Philadelphia printer, published a tract in Memoriam to her husband. In it is a description of Elizabeth Haddon Estaugh's personality and good works. He wrote, "Elizabeth Haddon was the most forceful woman in the district."

WHY HADDONFIELD?

Haddonfield at the time of the Revolutionary War had developed into the largest village and trade center in which is now Camden County. What stimulated the growth of a village at this particular site is an intriguing part of Haddonfield's early history. Unlike its neighbors the site possessed all the essential ingredients for the growth of a colonial village: tidal water for transportation, a fording place of a major waterway for highways, and streams that could be dammed to provide water power for mills.

From the first settlement in the 1680's to the Revolutionary War, almost 100 years later, virtually all transportation of goods in and out of the area was by means of flatboats floating on the tidal streams. Public landings were established near the head of tidewater where products were brought for shipment. The commercial benefits to the area adjacent to these landings grew as the population increased. The erection of mills utilizing the power of the flowing streams above tidewater further advanced the commercial advantages of the site of Haddonfield as the area settlers were obliged to come to its sawmills for lumber or gristmills to have their grains ground into meal or flour.

The fording place of the Cooper River above the tidal ebb and flow: the river was a place where Indian trails converged to cross the waterway, then branched out again in various directions. To the best of present knowledge the ford across the south branch of the Cooper River was about the middle of today's Evans

28

Pond. These ancient trails became the first system of roads used by the European settlers. The trail from Haddonfield was utilized as part of the route of the Great Road from Burlington to Salem laid out in 1681 by the General Assembly of West New Jersey. It was completed in 1686 and was known locally as the "Salem Road." The King's Highway did not become the road to Salem until after 1760 when a new route was surveyed utilizing King's Highway through Haddonfield to Market Street in Mount Ephraim and from that point continued to Salem by way of Woodbury and Swedesboro. This more convenient route replaced the original "Salem Road" with its Indian trail meanderings. The name King's Highway is a very recent designation. In 1713 it was called Queen's Road," in 1760 the "King's Road," in 1776 the "Salem Road," in 1820 "the road from Haddonfield to Mount Ephraim," and as late as 1910 it was called "Main Street."

A major factor, too, in the continued growth of the village, not shared by other villages, was the building of the Friend's Meeting House in 1721 at its location on Haddon Avenue, the road to Cooper's Ferry. These ferries located on the north end of today's Camden City, provided the most convenient crossing place from New Jersey to Philadelphia, which, by the mid-1700's, had become the largest business and cultural center in the American Colonies, providing a substantial market for all local products.

THE REVOLUTIONARY WAR

Upon the breaking out of the Revolutionary War the members of the Society of Friends in the colonies found themselves in a peculiar situation. The principles of non-resistance and passive obedience entered so largely into their faith and practice that it was not until after hostilities began that they were accused of sympathy with the loyal cause. But by far the larger number of Friends were on the side of the people, and rendered such aid and comfort as could be done consistent with their faith.

The last encampment of the Hessians, under Count Donop, before the battle of Red Bank, October 22, 1777, was in Haddonfield. This body of 1200 troops strong was encamped in the field near John Gill's house, the original house at what is now John Gill IV house, 343 King's Highway East. During the night of October 21, the headquarters of Count Donop were in this house, the largest and most elegant in the town. The next day the battle was fought, and Count Donop was mortally wounded, and died three days later.

During the war, the Hessians and American troops were often ranging through the town. After the battle of Red Bank, where Hessian troops were defeated, they returned to Haddonfield in detached bodies. The Friends Meeting House on Haddon Avenue was used as a hospital, and later by both armies. Many times during the war the people of Haddonfield and vicinity were harassed by troops from both armies, foraging for supplies. During the critical year of 1777, Haddonfield provided a safe meeting place at the "Old Tavern" (later named the Indian King) for the New Jersey legislators to conduct their affairs of state when they were routed by the British from one meeting place to another. Here events took place which shaped the history of New Jersey. Here the celebrated Generals of the War were quartered-Generals "Light Horse" Harry Lee, Nathaniel Greene, Anthony Wayne, Cavalry Commander Count Pulaski, and the Marquis de Lafayette, recovering from his wounds after the successful battle he fought with the enemy under Cornwallis, between Mt. Ephraim and Gloucester, November 25, 1777. His delightful and descriptive report of the battle to General Washington is dated *"Haddonfield, November, 1777."*

After having spent the most part of the day in making myself well acquainted with the certainty of the enemy's motions, I came pretty late into the Gloucester Road between the two creeks. I had ten light horse, almost one hundred fifty riflemen and two pickets of militia. Colonel Armand, Colonel Laumoy, and Cheviliers, Duplessis and Gimat were the Frenchmen with me. A scout of men under Duplessis went to ascertain how near to Gloucester were the enemy's first pickets, and they found at a distance of two miles and a half from that place a strong post of three hundred Hessians with field-pieces, and they engaged immediately. As my little reconnoitering party were all in fine spirits I supported them. We pushed the Hessians more than half a mile from the place where their main body had been, and we made them run very fast.

British reinforcements came twice to them, but very far from recovering their ground, they always retreated. The darkness of the night prevented us from pursuing

our advantage. After standing on the ground we had gained, I ordered them to return to Haddonfield. I take great pleasure in letting you know that the conduct of our soldiers was above all praise. I never saw men so merry, so spirited and so desirous to go on to the enemy, whatever force they might have, as the small party in this little fight.

*British: Killed 25 to 30   Lafayette: 1 Lt. Killed
           Wounded 25 to 30   5 Wounded*

Early Haddonfield was essentially a farming community. With large land holdings, farming became the favored occupation of the early settlers. Many of them introduced the most modern methods into their cultivation of the land. Their farms prospered and farmers like John Roberts, John Gill, Isaac Wood, David Roe, Ezra Bell and Thomas Redman were among the wealthiest men in the community. Haddonfield also became eminent for its physicians, lawyers and jurists. And wealthy merchants from Philadelphia built impressive "summer" homes in the "beautiful town" to enjoy "country living," away from the city.

The advent of the Camden and Atlantic Railroad in 1853 did much to change the character of Haddonfield. A few business firms conceived the idea that the railroad, the first to be built completely across the state to the ocean, bringing vast areas of southern New Jersey into productive use, would provide an economical means of cartage for their goods. Jackson Glass Works of Atco, John Lucas, paint manufacturer, Judge Porter of Waterford Glass, and William Coffin of Winslow Glass Works formed a corporation, bought the land and laid the tracks. The railroad brought in new trades and tradesmen who built modest but pleasing homes. Philadelphia merchants continued to build their mansions in this pleasant town with the convenience of railroad transportation to their business. The economic pressures also grew but the essential traditions and values of Quaker Haddonfield were not lost.

Note:

We are indebted to William W. Leap, historian and past president of the Camden County Historical Society, for his invaluable assistance in providing accurate information on the early history of Haddonfield. He is the author of the section, "Why Haddonfield," the most comprehensive account of the geographical advantages of the village which shaped its development. Also, to the late Elizabeth Hopkins Lenhart, local historian, for her charming profile of Elizabeth Haddon.

Kay-Shivers Houses, 1836

434-436 King's Highway East

Opposite: *The six over six pane window sash in reveal frames with paneled shutters define the early character of the house.*

These charming twin houses of the Federal period in Haddonfield bear the mark of architectural excellence identified with their builder, John Shivers, who built, among other fine houses in the town, the John Clement "Three Sisters" residences at 227-229-231 King's Highway East. John Shivers and his family lived in the larger section, and shortly thereafter built the twin houses to the west, 430-432.

The homes were built on land held by the John Kay family since 1710, when the land was bought by John Kay, one of the leading men of the early settlement. In 1685 he was elected to the General Assembly of the province of West New Jersey and also became one of the judges of the courts of the county. The houses have carried his name as a historical reference.

The distinctive features of these two and a half story twin houses are the stucco exterior, scored to simulate cut stone, the Federal style paired end wall chimneys, the curved pediment dormers, and the impressive Doric portico with fluted Greek Doric columns. Typical of John Shivers doorways, which he made a most important feature of the front facade, these have eight raised panels and beautiful lunette fanlights.

By the 1950's the four houses were in a state of decay, destined for commercial rezoning. The houses, 434-436, were restored by leading local architect, Herbert R. Leicht, who added the curved front entrance steps as the dwellings were built with the front yard well above the present level of King's Highway, cut through at a later date.

The twin houses to the west were restored in 1961-62 by owners Dexter and Helen Streeter completing the restoration of the original Federal period beauty of the four Shivers houses.

Above: *The paired end wall chimneys on the east side have an unusual half round window.*

Baptist Chapel, 1889

402 King's Highway East

This exquisite example of rural Gothic frame churches in New Jersey is one of the treasures of the Historic District. It was built in 1889 with funds raised by the woman's group known as the Baptist Social Circle, Inc. of the First Baptist Church of Haddonfield and named the John Sisty Memorial Chapel in memory of John Sisty, a Philadelphia merchant who was licensed to preach by the Mt. Holly Baptist Church in order to hold these exercises.

The mortuary chapel was needed to accommodate funerals at the adjoining Baptist Cemetery. Previously funerals had been held in private homes with the coffin maker acting as undertaker.

The Chapel was built on the site of the original Baptist Church building erected in 1818, demolished in 1852, and the site of the second Baptist edifice built in 1853 and torn down in 1885.

The land was purchased by the pioneer Baptists from the heirs of Elizabeth West, daughter of John Kay III, who was the grandson of John Kay I who came to West Jersey in 1680 and acquired large holds of land, including the 100 acres called the Lovejoy Triangle which ran along the south side of King's Highway East from Ellis Street to Cooper's Creek.

During World War II, Civil Defense classes for high school students were held in the Chapel. Although it has not been used for funerals for many years, the rear portion houses the cemetery's business office and records.

The charming bell tower on the slate roof, the pointed Gothic windows, the portico ornamented with lacy Victorian brackets in the gable, the simplicity and fine proportions exemplify the architectural features that made this rural Gothic Revival church style so popular in the 18th and 19th centuries.

Built right on the street front adjoining the old cemetery which extends several hundred feet on King's Highway, enclosed by hedged walls and stone piers at the entrance to the driveway, the Baptist Chapel and Cemetery present one of the most picturesque sites on King's Highway.

John Roberts Farm, 1816

344 King's Highway East

"I moved to Haddonfield because its historic character has been preserved, and the spacious old gardens that grace the Historic District are the closest thing to Virginia, where I lived for many years."
Della Mae Reutter, present owner

As one views this impressive brick mansion, the most important dwelling remaining in Haddonfield of the early Federal period, built in 1816 for "Master Farmer John Roberts," and its two-acre magnificent planned garden, it is difficult to imagine that at that time it was only a two-room house and the land was a truck farm, part of the 600 acres Roberts owned and extending to what is now Potter Street.

The original house, the part on the east side, had one room downstairs and one upstairs with a staircase leading to the second floor and a front entrance, features which still remain. The spacious downstairs room was used as a living room, dining room and kitchen and the original cooking fireplace with its massive Federal design mantel still dominates the room, now used as the formal dining room by its present owners, Mr. and Mrs. John G. Reutter.

The house was enlarged to its present size, a third floor with dormers added, about the period of 1830, judging from the exterior and interior architectural details which are distinctly of that late Federal period in Haddonfield. The Doric portico with its fluted Greek Doric columns supporting a full entablature ornamented with fine dentil detail was also an addition at this time. The second doorway on the west side leads to the "new" center hall and addition, matching the 1816 doorway, as does the design of the fanlights. An exquisitely carved iron grill adorns this door.

The paired end wall chimneys on the addition also match the paired chimneys on the 1816 east side, with that date embedded in in the brickwork, the date also appearing on the decorative leaderheads of the built-in gutters. The brick east wing supports the second floor open porch which was added in the twentieth century, as was the narrow two-story brick west wing. The charming picket fence with acorn finial posts, an important architectural feature of the house, has existed as far back as anyone in the town can remember.

Farmer Roberts was a man of means and an important personage in early Haddonfield history. In 1782, he became a member of the Friendship Fire Company (now the Haddonfield Fire Department), which had been organized in 1764, one of the oldest in the country. In 1803, he was one of the original nineteen subscribers to the Haddonfield Library Company. He is also remembered as one of the succession of owners of the "Upper Tavern," now the Indian King, which he bought for 900 pounds in 1805 from Samuel Deny and held during his lifetime which ended September 1, 1845. His grand homestead descended to his grandson, John K. Roberts whose children, Hannah E. Mitchell, John Morris Roberts and Harriet K. Roberts became the ultimate heirs of the John Roberts estate. John Morris Roberts was Haddonfield's first mayor.

Contemporary owners have made additions to the house with reverence for maintaining its architectural integrity. Present owners, Mr. and Mrs. John Reutter, gifted gardeners, have added a delightful greenhouse. Previous owner David Stern, then publisher of the Courier-Post and Philadelphia Record, added a library room in the rear, entered by the beautiful music room beyond the immense living room to the right of the center hall, the "new" part of the house.

Roberts-Mitchell House, 1865-1883

334 King's Highway East

I wanted an old house...an old house has so much character, all those Victorian details. The restoration has been so rewarding.

Mary Mack, Owner

This charming Gothic Revival, rural style house is another "Cinderella-restoration" story in the Historic District, transformed from its badly altered state to the Victorian beauty we enjoy today, by its present owners, Dr. Ronald and Mary Mack.

Their first step was to remove the old asbestos siding from the exterior walls and reveal and repair the original wood siding. The next big step was to restore the beautiful original front porch and side porch on the east side which had been removed in the 20th century to be replaced with an inappropriate Federal-style portico. Fortunately, the side porch on the west side had been preserved and served as a guide for the replication of the lacy cut out brackets and posts for the restored porches.

A nondescript pale yellow and white color scheme which had obscured the Victorian detailing gave way to an authentic 19th century color scheme of three colors, placed to accent the contrasts of body, trim and decoration. The original shutters, as the handsome paneled interior doors, found neglected and "abused" in the basement, were rescued by the Macks and restored to their pristine condition.

Note the two-story finely bracketed and paneled bays on this three-story house, the small curved windows in the steep gables, characteristic of the period, and the original standing seam tin roof, blessedly not replaced by a modern roof as was the case on roofs of many period houses.

The 1865 "country style" of this house is in sharp contrast to the 1816 Federal style elegant brick mansion next door to the East—the Roberts Homestead. But the two houses are related by ownership in the same family. The Roberts-Mitchell house was built by Hannah E. Mitchell, the daughter of the John K. Roberts who inherited the original John Roberts farm from his grandfather in 1841. Mrs. Mitchell, with her brother John Morris Roberts, the first mayor of Haddonfield, and sister Harriet K. Roberts were the ultimate heirs of the John Roberts estate.

The front parlor of the house was constructed about 1865; the addition to the rear has the date 1883 inscribed in the plaster found when old wallpaper was removed. Mrs. Mitchell also owned the Hartley tannery and house adjacent on the west side of her property, long since removed.

In later years this house fell into a state of disrepair and was used as a boarding house. Now it is a treasure in the town.

Restoration begins: the removal of asbestos siding and the later added inappropriate portico.

"Old End"
1743-1876

316 King's Highway East

Opposite: Very simple, understated Victorian details feature two-story bay windows on west side, plain pilasters as corner posts, modest brackets under heavy cornice overhang.

We strive to save our historic and architectural heritage simply because we have lived with it and it has become part of us. The presence of our physical past creates expectations and anticipations that are important parts of our daily lives.

> Robert Stipe,
> National Trust for Historic Preservation

This impressive Italianate style house, the front part of which you see on King's Highway, was built on the original 1743 home, a portion of which served as a delightful seventeen foot square "Keeping Room," overlooking one of the loveliest gardens in Haddonfield. Until recently, this was the home of celebrated local historians, the late Jesse and Edna Haydock. The Haydocks bought the house in 1915 from Deborah Morris Roberts, widow of John K. Roberts who built the house in 1876 on land originally part of his grandfather's farm. With the Haydock's purchase, the last piece of the John Roberts farmland went out of the Roberts family.

To build this grand house, Deborah Roberts had to move three small colonial houses on the property, houses that had been built in 1743 and moved to the Roberts site from just west of the Indian King in 1836 to make way for the three brick John Clement houses now standing. She used one of the little houses as her kitchen in the new house, one she moved near the property line for her garden tools, and the third house was moved to Ellis Street. This one was saved and restored as the earliest dwelling extant in Haddonfield by the Historical Society which relocated it next to Greenfield Hall, Society headquarters.

The 1876 house was built in the grand Victorian fashion of the time with characteristic porch across the entire front. During the Colonial Revival period, the porch was removed and replaced by a formal portico entrance with fluted Doric columns and classic moldings. The Victorian double doors were replaced with a handsome cherry and mahogany paneled door from an early Philadelphia house. The original sidelights and ornamented fan light remain.

Edna Haydock died in 1985 at the age of 103. She had lived in this home for seventy years and maintained it and her beautiful garden with impeccable care. She was dedicated to historic preservation for Haddonfield, a forceful presence in fighting for it during its turbulent beginnings. She was one of the incorporators of the Haddonfield Preservation Society in 1967.

The Italianate Style, 1860

306 King's Highway East

Country residences in the Italian style are becoming more and more popular. Its great pliability of design, its facile adaptation to our wants and habits, together with its finished, elegant, and picturesque appearance give it precedence over every other.

Samuel Sloan,
"The Model Architect," 1852

This handsome example of the Italianate style of Victorian architecture in Haddonfield, a style which produced several of the town's most beautiful "villas," is true to the Italianate characteristics—"a rectangular (almost square) two or three story house with very wide eaves usually supported by large brackets, a low pitch roof topped with a cupola. A central one-bay porch or long porches also are evident in the style."

Unfortunately, the cupola and elegantly designed porch were removed in the 1950's (see old photo) but many of the original architectural details have been preserved. The six-paneled double entrance door of chestnut with its age-old patina is one of the most beautiful in the Historic District, as is the double-bracketed bay window on the west side, a delightful and dominant feature of the 30 ft. living room.

The one-story addition on the left of the building was used as an office by Dr. Bowman H. Shivers who was an early tenant of the home which was probably built as a rental property. Dr. Shivers began the practice of homeopathy in Haddonfield in 1864 and one entered his office from a three-step circular portico. Later the door was replaced by a window and the steps removed.

The land upon which the house was built was part of the original John Roberts Farm, and was titled to William Coffin Shinn by John K. Roberts in 1857. Shinn was a noted local builder in the contracting business and it is likely he built this house as he built several other elegant houses in the town.

After Shinn's death in 1874, his widow Louisa Jane, sold the house in 1879 to Samuel Clement, descendent of the distinguished early Clement family, and her future son-in-law, for the sum of $6,750. The Clements sold the property in 1918 to Maud Winkler who conducted music classes there and was a gifted gardener, creating,

according to surviving neighbors, one of the most beautiful gardens in the town. In 1945, the house was sold to Wallace Bourne, and later the interior was altered for multi-tenant use, housing the music conservatory of Marie Dager, a noted musician.

When Jeanne and Don Jackson bought the house in 1971, they restored the building to its original single family use and created a picture-book garden from what had become an ugly, neglected backyard. Some of Maud Winkler's rare plants were given to the Jacksons from a neighbor who had received them from Miss Winkler.

This elegantly designed porch was removed in the 1950's and replaced with a Federal-style portico. It had a beautiful ornamented cornice, decorative detail on the square columns with unusual inset panels, and bold multi-moldings. The Historic District Ordinance was enacted in 1971 to preserve such significant architectural elements on the town's historic houses.

Judge John Clement House, 1852-1743

264 King's Highway East

The preference in architecture of Andrew Jackson Downing, America's leading landscape architect, was for the Gothic Revival style. "Those who love shadow and the sentiment of antiquity and repose will find most pleasure in the quiet tone which prevails in the Gothic style."

Seven generations of the same family have owned and lived in this house. The handsome Gothic Revival mansion we see today was built in 1852 by John Clement Jr., on the site of the original house built in 1743 by his granduncle, Jacob Clement, a tanner, at the time of his marriage to Elizabeth Tiley. Jacob Clement operated a tannery here which continued after his death in 1784 until 1812. Inheriting the house from his father John Clement Sr., nephew of Jacob Clement, the son, desiring a grander house of a design very much in vogue at the time, removed the front of the original structure, moved it to a site on Potter Street, but retained the rear portion as a commodious kitchen which is part of the house to this day.

The history of the house becomes more and more interesting with each generation. John Clement Sr., born in 1769, died 1855, became one of the most prominent citizens in Haddonfield. He had won considerable recognition as a surveyor of land and for his settlement of disputed boundaries and division of real estate. He held numerous civic and judicial posts and became the first Postmaster of Haddonfield on March 22, 1803, appointed by President Thomas Jefferson. He also built several houses in the town which are considered historically important, including the three brick houses for his daughters next to the Indian King.

This illustrious Clement passed on to his son his exceptional knowledge and experience. John Clement Jr. lived up to his father's achievements as a civic and judicial leader, and in 1864 was appointed Lay Judge of the Court of Errors and Appeals. Judge John Clement left an important legacy to the town, not only in his historic house but in his 442 page book, "The First Settlers of Newton," published in 1887, an exhaustive sketch of his native town from the colonial period to 1862.

The new home Judge John Clement built embodied the excellence of mid-nineteenth century construction. The formal vestibule, the wide pine floor boards, ceilings twelve feet high with deep molded cornices, and venetian blinds with hand-carved double valances, are a few of the architectural details which project the status of the Clements, as does the exterior. There is no more decorative and entrancing portico in the town as the one here with its original striped curved tin roof, jig-sawn drop finial bargeboards, chamfered posts supporting three-centered Tudor arches with trefoil cut out spandrels. The central cross gable in the steep slate roof also has elaborate jig-sawn bargeboards with scallops and drop finials. People stop, stare, and find pleasure in such exceptional and artistic craftsmanship of the nineteenth century.

In contemporary history this was the home of Thomas Smith Hopkins, born in 1884 at Birdwood, a descendant of the John Estaugh Hopkins family, who married Louisa Albertson Clement. Thomas Hopkins was a brilliant local historian and left many valuable historical papers for posterity. He served as president of the local committee for the care of the Indian King Tavern, appointed by the State, after the tavern was purchased as a state museum in 1903. His book, co-authored with Walter Cox, "Colonial Furniture of West Jersey," is now a collector's treasure. His daughter, Elizabeth Hopkins Lenhart, born 1913, died in May, 1990, followed in the family tradition of distinguished historians. She was official historian of the Preservation Society and in the forefront of its efforts to achieve historic preservation for her native town.

Aspden-Champion-Blackwood House, 1760-1846

254 King's Highway East

One of Haddonfield's finest early period houses.

Louis H. Goettelmann, AIA

The interesting families associated with this house, the significance of its architecture, and its preservation as a private residence over 230 years, make this dwelling "a jewel in the crown," of the architectural history of Haddonfield. Three men of prominence owned and lived in this house. Matthias Aspden, who built the Indian King Tavern in 1750, built this house as his residence in 1760. It was considered at that time to be the most expensive house in the village. The land belonged to Elizabeth Haddon Estaugh who in 1746 bought it from Timothy Matlack and David Elwell. When Matthias Aspden purchased a part of the four acres, he built what was recorded as a "fine mansion."

Aspden died in 1765, leaving the property to his son Matthias Jr., a wealthy shipping merchant in Philadelphia, who was declared a Tory during the Revolution. His property, including the house, was confiscated, but after the war he was exonerated and the property returned to him in 1786.

Shortly thereafter the house was sold to Thomas Champion, a well-to-do tailor, whose grandfather, John Champion had distinguished the family by establishing a ferry over Cooper's Creek in 1702, the beginning of the Old Egg Harbor Road. Thomas lived in the house until his death, when it passed to his son Samuel.

Why should this "fine mansion" be sold at Sheriff's sale on June 6, 1840? No one knows, but one can surmise it was the changing fortunes of the Champion family. It was the good fortune of the town that the new purchaser was another eminent personage, Dr. Benjamin F. Blackwood, born in 1800, a graduate in medicine at the University of Pennsylvania in 1828, and the husband of Mary Ann Hopkins, daughter of William Estaugh Hopkins, illustrious original owner of "Birdwood."

In 1846, Dr. Blackwood added some luxurious features to the house. The new brick front still retained the colonial character of the original "fine mansion," with the same six over six pane windows and the beautiful three-panel shutters. One enters the house through the simple colonial portico and paneled double doors to a center hall, remarkable for its stairway which winds all the way to the third floor, its newel post and bannister made of rare golden tiger stripe maple. The 1846 living room, dining room and upstairs rooms are extraordinarily large. The architectural details are of the classic revival period with a simple square black marble fireplace mantel in the living room which can be found in other great houses of the period in Haddonfield.

Dr. Blackwood died in 1866, leaving his property to his two unmarried daughters, the second of whom passed away in 1891. In 1902, the house was purchased by George B. England. His daughter Elizabeth, born March 6, 1897, became a Collingswood schoolteacher and married Louis F. Mack, an electrical engineer. The couple made the Englands' home their home for the rest of their lives. Elizabeth died at the age of 93 on July 7, 1990. She often expressed her love for the historic house and maintained it and the beautiful garden almost to the end of her days. She was an ardent supporter of historic preservation and a member of the Preservation Society for twenty years.

Above: *Focal point of garden is this large gazebo with interesting copper roof and lattice work, somewhat Moorish Victorian architectural style, indicating it was added here later.*

Guard House, 1732

258-260 King's Highway East

"This house built in colonial times was used during the Revolutionary War as a Guard House for persons suspected of aiding the British cause and brought to trial before the Council of Safety then meeting in the Indian King."

Bronze tablet erected by
Daughters of American Revolution

Many marks of early workmanship still remain in the two attached earlier buildings, #258 and #260, built by Timothy Matlack in 1732, who came to Haddonfield in 1726 and conducted a brewery business across the street about where the Indian King Tavern now stands. Some of the beams are handhewn and have wooden pegs. The house at the west of the three, #256, was added about 100 years later.

The house at #258, at the center of the three, originally the home of Timothy Matlack, is frequently mentioned during the year 1777, as it was used as a guard house for persons suspected of aiding the British cause and brought to trial before the Council of Safety, then meeting at the Indian King. A report of the guard at that place, dated May 23, 1777, shows that three officers and nine privates were on duty; four sentries in the daytime and two by night. The prisoners at that time consisted of four men taken at sea, six enemies to the states, and sixteen prisoners of war, the names of whom were given. Andrew Invirie was Lieutenant in charge on that day.

The two original houses are built of brick, a material readily available in the colonial period. The simple shed dormers in the hip roof are an early design throughout the region, as are the eight over eight pane window sash. The three-columned portico was added in later years.

Situated on King's Highway opposite the historic 1750 Indian King Tavern, these colonial buildings which embody the distinctive characteristics of an early method of construction, recall a significant period in Haddonfield history.

Dr. Napoleon Bonaparte Jennings House, 1857

236 King's Highway East

Opposite: *One of the town's charming examples of the Gothic Revival Cottage style.*

Dr. Jennings was possessed of a singularly genial nature, which overflowed in kindness to all and gained for him the universal good will of the community in which he lived and practiced for nearly thirty years.

Prowell's History of Camden County, N.J.

One of the few remaining fine old early Victorian residences on King's Highway East, the oldest settled section of the village, illustrates the sophisticated architectural features that gave rich character to the Gothic Revival Cottage style. The house was built by a Dr. Hall in 1857 and had no bay windows or porch. It had an enchanting ornamented front portico with deep lacy cut out facing and a striped tin porch roof, a much admired common practice when the roof was visible. The house was purchased in 1867 by Dr. Napoleon Bonaparte Jennings, a graduate of Jefferson Medical College in 1856, who immediately entered upon the practice of medicine in Haddonfield, where he soon gained the confidence of the community for his professional and social accomplishments which attained for him one of the largest practices ever secured by a physician in West Jersey.

He lived and practiced here with his son, William, born in 1865; all six of his other children were born in this house. It may have been the need for more space for his growing family, or the fire that destroyed part of the west side of the house, or simply while rebuilding to "update" the house in the architectural vogue of the time, that resulted in the major changes he made.

The two-story bay windows were added, with colored glass panes, and a full porch across the front took the place of the striped roof portico. The new porch has its own delightful details — spandrel brackets on chamfered posts and graceful turned balusters. The Gothic influence is seen in the pointed dormers, the deep front gable with scalloped vergeboards and windows with pedimented architraves — all features of the original house. The front steps had elaborate iron grillwork, now gone, but the entrance into a vestibule with beautiful frosted glass doors leading to a center hall still remain.

The Jennings property went all the way back to what is now Harding Avenue, a one block street. In the garden were planted fruit trees, a grape arbor, a vegetable garden and a spectacular hedge of white and purple lilacs to screen the barn and barnyard. The garden is now cut up for parking lots.

After Dr. Jennings' death in 1885, his widow, Mary Browning Jennings, sold the home to her son, William, and moved in with her bachelor brother, Isaac Browning, who had a large home at 35 King's Highway West, one of the several demolished when Linden Avenue was cut through. Dr. William Jennings died in 1928 and his widow lived in the house until 1929. In 1946, Dr. Francis L. Rossell and his wife, Thelma, purchased the house as a home and physician's office. Tragedy struck when their son was killed in Vietnam. The beautiful holly tree planted on the east side of the house was a gift of the Haddon Fortnightly in his memory. The very lovely and celebrated dwelling is now a professional office.

Original house before additions of bay windows and porch

Reeves-Glover House, 1813-1835

232 King's Highway East

It has been fairly claimed that American building of those years, the so-called Federal period, was at least equal in merit to that of any nation in the world.

History of Notable American Houses,
American Heritage

One of the most beautiful, architecturally significant houses of the Federal period in Haddonfield, the Reeves-Glover House was built in two parts, as were many other houses of this period. The east wing was built by William Alexander in 1813, on the site of an earlier frame house owned by Lydia Bates. Later it was owned by Benjamin Cooper of the notable Camden County Cooper family. When Samuel M. Reeves purchased it in 1835, he added the west wing with apparently great care to match the original east wing. Samuel Reeves' business was conveyancing, handling of deeds, and similar matters. His granddaughter married George B. Glover and she inherited the house. It remained in the Glover family for many years and was known as the Glover homestead. Despite alterations that were made in the 1960's to the front facade when the dwelling became a shop specializing in Williamsburg reproductions, and later, offices, the incredibly beautiful interior architectural details have been preserved—the fireplaces in every room, the elegant woodwork and stairways. On the exterior, the original front windows with six over six panes were replaced by two divided light bulk windows, but the handsome paneled front entrance door with original fanlight has been preserved.

The alterations could not destroy the intrinsic character of one of the finest early 19th century brick mansions on historic King's Highway.

Above: *The double chimneys, curved dormers and second floor windows and shutters of the 1813-1835 building have not been altered. The pent eave and the first floor bulk windows are 1962 alterations. The beauty and stature of the historic brick building, despite alterations, enhance the early streetscape.*

John Clement Houses, 1836

227, 229, 231 King's Highway East

"The Three Sisters" houses were built by John Clement for his three daughters by my father, John Shivers.
Sara Shivers Murray, 1929

The beautiful brickwork, the elegant rhythm of the window placement, the curved pediment dormers which marked the houses of the Federal period are no better displayed in Haddonfield than in these three attached houses, built by John Clement, Sr., a prominent local citizen, for his three daughters. "Squire" Clement, as he was known, was a surveyor, the Collector of Revenue for Gloucester County, and Haddonfield's first Postmaster, appointed in 1803 by President Thomas Jefferson. He chose John Shivers, local master builder with a practical knowledge of architecture, to construct the houses in the style of the young Republic declaring its architectural independence from Georgian England.

The previous buildings on these lots were small one and a half story eighteenth century rustic frame dwellings which were removed to other locations to make way for the Clement houses. One of these colonial dwellings was built by Samuel Mickle and was moved to Ellis Street, then moved in 1965 by the Historical Society next door to Greenfield Hall and restored for its historic significance as the earliest dwelling extant in Haddonfield.

When the new houses were completed, Squire Clement intended #231 (next to the Indian King) for his daughter, Amelia who married Joshua Paul B. Browning; the house at #229 was for daughter Abbe, who was married to William Doughden; and the house at #227 was for daughter Sara, unmarried at the time, and so became a rental property for a few years until Sara married Griffith Hopkins. The daughter of John Shivers purchased the house at #227 in 1917 and her 1929 manuscript has provided us with an excellent history of the Clement houses.

When they were built, each house had a basement kitchen, two rooms on the first floor, three on the second and three on the third. In those days, families usually ate in their kitchens except when entertaining guests in the back parlor, which, separated from the front parlor by folding doors, became the dining room. The attic floor was open across the three houses so that the sisters had indoor access to each other's home. The homes had four open fireplaces; one in each parlor and in each second story bedroom. "The mantel pieces were of wood with wonderfully good lines, those downstairs being painted black."

Alterations have changed the original face of the entrances to these buildings. The later added Victorian porch on #229 is obviously out of character but not the doorway at #231, which, though not original, is in the Federal style with a pedimented six panel door, a beautiful fanlight designed in a swag muntin pattern, paneled jambs and fluted pilasters. The doorway came from a Federal house in Philadelphia found by Herbert R. Leicht, noted local architect and president of the Historical Society, when that building was its headquarters for more than twenty years. The Doric portico at #227 may be original as it is appropriate to the period and style of the house, reminiscent of the three Captain's houses on Nantucket Island which were built for his three daughters. The three houses are now offices and the Historic District Ordinance preserves these architectural gems from further alteration.

Indian King Tavern, 1750

233 King's Highway East

Opposite: *Original building now restored was built in two sections: eastern section, two and a half stories; western section, three stories, 12 over 12 window sash in plank frames on second and third floors. Two entrance doors: one led to tap room, closed to ladies; the other to public dining room.*

Whatever the village is the center of the inn is the center of the village.

A historian has written, "No other building or site in Haddonfield is so intrinsically woven into the fabric of its early history and the events that helped shape the history of New Jersey as the Indian King." The Indian King Tavern, a state-owned historic site since 1903, is the focus of the social, economic and political life of Haddonfield's colonial history. Symposiums are held on the history and significance of the Indian King, and no history of Haddonfield is complete without it.

Built in 1750 by Matthias Aspden, a wealthy Philadelphia merchant and shipowner, it became the scene of important events during the Revolutionary War. On January 3, 1777, the New Jersey legislators, routed by the British from one meeting place to another, decided on the public house at Haddonfield as a safe place to conduct their affairs of state. On May 19, 1777, the New Jersey Assembly, in session at the Indian King, approved adoption of the Great Seal of New Jersey, a copy of which hangs in the tavern hall. A few months later, on September 20, 1777, the Assembly enacted a law substituting the word "State" for "Colony," in all commission, writs, and indictments.

Celebrated Generals of the War chose to quarter here as a "most commodious and hospitable house." Seen about town were Generals "Light Horse" Harry Lee, Nathaniel Greene, Anthony Wayne, the dashing Polish Cavalry Commander, Count Pulaski, and the twenty-year old Marquis de Lafayette, recovering from his wounds, after the successful battle he fought with the enemy under Cornwallis, between Mt. Ephraim and Gloucester, November 25, 1777. His delightful and descriptive report of the battle to General Washington, dated "Haddonfield, November 25, 1777" is reprinted on page 29

Another illustrious person associated with the Indian King is Dolley Madison who became First Lady of the White House when her husband James Madison was elected President in 1804. As Dorathea Payne, living in Quaker simplicity with her parents in Philadelphia, the 18-year old "Dolley" frequently visited her uncle Hugh Creighton, the innkeeper of the Indian King from 1777 to 1790, after quieter times returned to Quaker Haddonfield. The pretty and popular Dolley enjoyed the dances and social activity which were centered in the village inn. On the second floor of the tavern is the charming "Dolley Madison Bedroom," though Dolley never slept at the inn, but stayed with the Peyton family nearby. Young single girls didn't bed at taverns.

By its strategic location on the great road that was the artery to Cooper's Creek, a principal highway of commerce in the region, the tavern became a popular stopping place for commercial travelers and wayfarers from near and far. It is said that as many as forty teams gathered at one time in the stable yard.

The building you see today has undergone at least six major alterations, and some additions. The original building was a small frame one built by Timothy Matlock as a store, to which he soon added some other buildings, including "malt house, brew house, and still house." When Matthias Aspden acquired the property he built a solid brick building, large enough to accommodate his residence and a commodious tavern and inn.

The Indian King's lively tavern days ended in 1873 when the town elected to prohibit the sale of liquor, which remains today. It became "The American House," a boarding house and ice cream parlor. In the late 19th century, the colonial building was "Victorianized" with a Victorian porch across the front. The old brick was covered with stucco which has not been removed. It soon was abandoned and fell into decay, to be rescued, at the initiative of local citizens, by the purchase of the State on June 15, 1903, which undertook its restoration, and appointed a commission of prominent local citizens for the "Care and Management of the Old Tavern House." The restoration by the architectural firm of Arthur H. Brockie in Philadelphia embellished the exterior, adding a pent roof over the first floor, so that it more nearly resembles the architectural style of old Philadelphia taverns. It is now a tourist attraction, visited by many people from many states and many countries.

Above: *The Ballroom of the Indian King where Governor William Livingston met with the New Jersey legislators on September 20, 1777, when the document was drawn changing New Jersey from "colony" to "state."*

Above: *Kitchen and Keeping Room of the Indian King with cooking fireplace, where the innkeeper, his family and servants ate their meals. On the table is a display of pottery made in Haddonfield by Wingarden Brothers.*

Peyton House, 1906

247 King's Highway East

A return to America's past...Colonial Revival was an excellent thing for American architecture. The result was a purification of the work and an increase of simplicity and chastity in American taste.

History of Notable American Houses,
American Heritage

At the turn of the century in Haddonfield and elsewhere, the enthusiasm for the over-ornamentation of nineteenth century Victorian styles waned and the vogue for the simplicity of the "Colonial" style grew. It was part of a wider revival of interest in all aspects of the early American scene, colonial furniture and furnishings and decorative arts. A pleasing aspect of the Colonial Revival Peyton House is that, placed among the eighteenth and nineteenth century buildings on King's Highway East, it is not out of place. The house, now offices, is only a few doors from the 1750 Indian King Tavern.

This large and imposing dwelling, named after Colonel Jesse E. Peyton, a leading figure in the town who lived in an earlier house on the site, was built, after his death, by his daughter Jane and son-in-law, Charles H. Hillman. He had a street cut through next to the property, naming it Colonial Avenue, and moved the old Peyton home to what is now 33 Colonial Avenue, making two houses from the one.

The original house, built by Joseph Bates about 1815, was the home for many years of Dr. Bowman Hendry, the most illustrious and beloved physician in Haddonfield history. After Dr. Hendry's death, the house was bought by Colonel Jesse E. Peyton, "a Kentucky gentleman," a progressive and enterprising resident, one of the promoters of the Centennial Exposition of 1876. In the 1850's he founded a bold enterprise, Hendry Hall, near Potter and Main, named after his friend Dr. Charles H. Hendry, son of Bowman Hendry. It was a place for lectures, musicales, and other cultural events. Unfortunately, it did not succeed financially, and was forced to close.

The Hillmans ended their days in the new house. It became part of the Peyton estate and was sold at auction in 1945 to its present owners, Henry D. Bean and Sons.

The design of this dwelling was very much favored by architects and builders of the "Colonial Revival" house. In 1896, the Ladies' Home Journal published a model design for a "Colonial House," very similar to the Peyton House. Both have the important portico entrance surmounted by a prominent balustrade and a side porch with simple columns and matching balustrade. The colonial-style triangular dormers are the same, as is the symmetry of the building, with its very large center hall, leading to two parlors, right and left of the hall. The facade of the Peyton House has not been altered and most of the interior architectural details have been preserved. It still maintains its original imposing residential character in the historic streetscape.

Above: *The revival of the colonial style which swept the country is exemplified in this 1906 Peyton House.*

Hendry-Pennypacker House, 1834

255 King's Highway East

The Federal style flourished in the early decades of the new nation. Federal-style buildings are found throughout the cities and towns of the eastern seaboard. Door and window openings were beautifully scaled and articulated, frequently incorporating fan and oval forms.

Preservation Press,
National Trust for Historic Preservation

One of the most beautiful, elegant houses remaining of the glorious Federal period in Haddonfield was built by one of its most distinguished citizens, Dr. Charles D. Hendry, son of Dr. Bowman Hendry, the most illustrious physician in Haddonfield history.

Charles Hendry was born in Haddonfield on May 8, 1809, and after graduating from the University of Pennsylvania in 1832, entered his father's practice, succeeding him after his death. It was only then that he was able to put into practice his advanced and popular ideas of medicine which his conservative father had frowned on.

Following the religious views of his family he contributed much toward the building of the Episcopal Church in Haddonfield, and was elected one of the vestrymen on April 20, 1843. Also through his efforts, the Camden County Medical Society was organized and he served as its president in 1852-1853. As his health declined, he abandoned his practice and returned to Philadelphia in 1865; he died in 1869.

The house passed through several ownerships until it was purchased in the early twentieth century by another outstanding citizen, James Lane Pennypacker, born in Philadelphia in 1855, and after graduation from Harvard College and entering the book publishing business in Boston and Philadelphia, moved to Haddonfield with his wife, Grace Fisher Coolidge of Dedham, Mass. where their five children were born. Mr. Pennypacker was a guiding light in the civic and cultural affairs of the community. His book "Verse and Prose," published by the Historical Society of Haddonfield in 1936, is a literary man's view of the village, its people, its local history and the natural world around him.

Offices now occupy the historic building but its public face is still the elegant private residence of Dr. Charles Hendry and James Lane Pennypacker. The two and one half story structure is built of Flemish Bond brickwork. The original Federal-style features are intact—the pairs of end wall chimneys with the finely made balustrade at roof flat; the two triangular pedimented dormers with six over six window sash, the standing seam tin roof with built-in gutters and molded box cornice; the recessed panel shutters and stone lintels over the cellular windows. A most noteworthy feature of the house is the front and side doors with eight raised panels, the leaded glass transom in a beautiful diamond and oval design, framed by Doric columns and topped with a triangular pediment. One enters the house by marble steps and a handsome wrought iron railing. The only alteration to the front facade is a semi-enclosed small porch added on the wing in the twentieth century to accommodate a doctor's office.

The Haddon Fortnightly, 1857

301 King's Highway East

Opposite: *Remodeled in 1936, the extended front is supported by columns of the Classic Revival period.*

This landmark building, listed in the State and National Register of Historic Places is now the home of the Haddon Fortnightly, organized in 1894, a member club of the New Jersey State Federation of Women's Clubs. The building has undergone several architectural changes since it was first built in 1857 as the United Methodist Church, its place of worship for 54 years when a larger Gothic stone church was built on Warwick Road. In 1911, the church sold the property to Americus R. Underdown, a Haddonfield resident, for a meeting place for the Artisan's Order of Mutual Protection. Renamed "Artisans' Hall," the building was remodeled, losing its church identity with the removal of the beautiful old church steeple.

Mr. Underdown died in 1922 and the building was destined for demolition. It was rescued by the Haddonfield Civic Association with the help of the Fortnightly women, to preserve it as a town meeting place. In January, 1931, the Haddon Fortnightly purchased the building from the Civic Association for $19,679.05, financing this in part by the sale of bonds. In March, the Fortnightly engaged a prominent local architect, Ellery K. Taylor, to prepare plans for the remodeling and beautification of the Hall. The plans included bringing the front of the building forward nine feet to provide a spacious foyer with two elegant staircases on either side leading to the auditorium upstairs. Thus, the original entrance doorway, which old photos show was framed with Doric columns and a pediment above, in the style of the Federal period, was removed and replaced with the existing unornamented doorway. All the windows which had been opaque were replaced with clear glass. The four column portico was a prominent addition, and probably was an attempt to identify the building with the Classic Revival period.

With the addition of a new kitchen, the old church kitchen was remodeled into an attractive tea room. A fireplace was added, the mantel a copy of the mantel that was in the house at Seventh and Market Streets in Philadelphia, where Thomas Jefferson worked on the draft of the Declaration of Independence.

Throughout its 97 years, the Fortnightly has supported local groups working to improve the community, including, in 1970-71, its successful efforts in the enactment of the Haddonfield Historic District Ordinance.

The clubhouse is a lively place today with programs, meetings, dinners, antique shows and exhibits, not only for the community but as a gracious and spacious place for receptions held by outside parties who appreciate the historic ambience of the building.

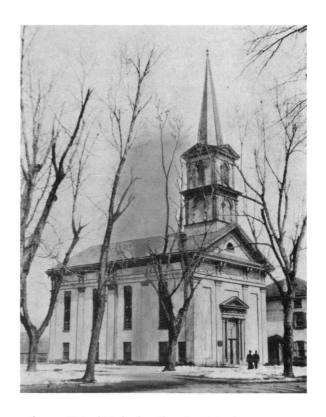

Above: *United Methodist Church original building before remodeling in 1911 and 1936.*

62

Shivers-French-Tatem House, 1758

309 King's Highway East

The brickwork of the English colonists in the Southern portion of the Province (New Jersey) is unexcelled and probably unequalled in America, though most of the dwellings are small.

New Jersey Architecture,
Lars de Lagerberg, 1956

The colonial origins of this three-story historic brick dwelling which we see and admire today, one of the earliest remaining on King's Highway East, go back to the land which was part of the Haddon-Estaugh plantation, bought by John Haddon from Richard Matthews in 1689. After a succession of transfers of ownership, it was bought in 1758 by John Shivers, a farmer, whose grandson John Shivers became one of Haddonfield's most prominent builders. It was an ideal location for farming as the property ran back to Hopkins Pond, giving the cows and livestock access to the water. The property ran west to what is now Haddon Avenue and east to within 100 feet of Evergeen Lane.

John Shivers built the first house on the property. It was of brick construction, two rooms wide and one room deep. Marks on the third-floor plaster show the house to have been two stories high, with an "A" roof loft. This was later raised to make two third-floor rooms with used lumber from another old house. It is not known when the rear of the house was added, but there remains a very early style door with a sliding panel opening into the garden. Some of the flooring is of swamp cedar, the mining of which was one of the early industries in southern New Jersey.

Haddonfield residents recall this house when the brick was covered with stucco, probably put on when the third floor was erected. In 1962, the owner of the house, Joseph Tatem, who inherited it from his father and grandfather, Joseph B. Tatem, who purchased the house in 1868 with a King's Highway frontage to a depth of 244 feet, undertook the mammoth job of removing the stucco and restoring the beautiful Flemish bond brick.

Upon removal of the stucco, Joe Tatem found several interesting details of the original building. The brick had been filled in perpendicularly where the second floor joists had protruded to support the pent roof, now removed. Much of the "belt course" as well as the "water-table" were intact. The two-story east side of the house has unusual matched frame boards. The entrance on King's Highway is through a simple Doric column portico, capped with a modillion cornice and entablature, framing the original six-panel door with raised panels, and an exceptionally lovely rectangular transom in an elliptical and diamond muntin design.

An important architectural feature of the house is the handsome wood fence across the frontage extending the entire length of the property along King's Highway. An enchanting high lattice screen with oval window, and posts with elegant vase finials, connect the house to the fence.

The house, referred to through the years as the Charles French house, highlights the ownership of Charles and Sabilla French, the last residents to have lived in the house during its colonial years. They sold the house in 1785, and have the distinction of being the parents of Elizabeth French who in 1841 married John Gill IV, and became the mistress of Greenfield Hall.

"Greenfield Hall," 1841

John Gill IV House,
343 King's Highway East

To the manners of a gentleman was united a sympathetic heart, thus insuring to those who had business with him a readiness to render them any service which was his power. A reliable friend, a thorough business man, an influential citizen and a person of enlarged and benevolent views, he was beloved and respected wherever known.

John Gill—Prowell's History
of Camden County, 1886

This stately mansion, its architecture borrowing the formal Georgian Colonial look in America, was built by John Gill IV as a wedding present for his intended bride, Elizabeth French of Moorestown. It was the third house built by a member of the Gill family at this location. Desiring to build a more gracious and spacious house for his new bride, John Gill tore down the previous house built by his grandfather in 1747. All that remains of the 1747 house is the portion on the east side of the present building which contains the "little room" and the servants' quarters above, now used as the Library in the Historical Society headquarters.

The first John Gill to build on this land was a cousin of Elizabeth Haddon Estaugh from whom he purchased 143 acres extending from Cooper's Creek westward to Meeting House Road (Haddon Avenue), along both sides of a small stream which, many years later, was dammed to form the present Hopkins Pond.

John Gill I came to the new world from England about 1705 and built, according to accounts, "a small hip-roofed frame building long since torn down." He was an educated man, which was an exception at that time, a surveyor, an accountant and a member of the religious Society of Friends. After the death of John Estaugh, Elizabeth's husband, he became the attorney and advisor to Elizabeth Estaugh, a service he performed for several other residents of the area.

It was in the house of John Gill II, son and heir, which he built in 1747, that an incident worth noting occurred during the American Revolution. On Tuesday evening, October 21, 1777, while the British occupied Philadelphia, Count Emil Kurt Donop, commanding 2,000 of his Hessian troops, stopped in Haddonfield on their way to Fort Mercer. The soldiers bivouacked in the fields near what is now Hopkins Pond and Count Donop made his headquarters at the home of John Gill, the most commodious house in town. The following morning the Hessians advanced to Fort Mercer and the Battle of Red Bank ensued. The Hessians were defeated and Count Donop's visit to the Gill house was recorded by Judge John Clement, "in John Gill's house Donop had his headquarters, and though the owner was an Elder among Friends, yet the urbanity and politeness of the German soldier so won upon him, that he was kindly remembered ever after."

Upon the death of John Gill II, in 1796, the house passed to his son, John Gill III, whose wife, Ann Smith of Burlington, was responsible for the design of the garden at Greenfield Hall, noted for its beauty. Many of the boxwood bushes remaining date from that time.

John Gill III died in 1838 and his son John Gill IV inherited the property. Born July 9, 1795, he had been reared on the homestead farm as a farmer, fond of his occupation. He was always seeking for improvement in the means to increase the yield of the soil and less labor by the application of machinery. The Gill farm homestead, located on what is now Lane of Acres, was restored by Mr. and Mrs. Edwin Pearson with the guidance of Herbert Leicht, restoration architect.

When his father died, John Gill IV, now a widower, moved to the Gill mansion on King's Highway. On April 15, 1841, he began work on the new house for his betrothed, which was completed on October 15, 1841. On October 21 he married Elizabeth French.

As we read of the many superior architectural features of this house (which follows), it is even more remarkable that they remain unaltered by the aging of time or the changes of man.

"Greenfield Hall," 1841

John Gill IV House
343 King's Highway East

Opposite: *Six over six window panes in reveal frames with recessed panel shutters are colonial features. (Historic American Buildings Survey Plan)*

The Architecture — The Georgian Look

It was an age when gentlemen took an interest in architecture, with the noble example of Thomas Jefferson. An age when wherever wealth was concentrated, Georgian architecture flourished, when the new style of Christopher Wren, the English architect most responsible for the style's development in England made its colonial debut and the Georgian manner became the main aesthetic force behind the best American houses.

Fortunately, for the quality of our Colonial architecture, there were many able artisans who could come over to interpret the style for which he was famous, and a host of builder's handbooks to guide the workmen here. One such handbook was published in Philadelphia in 1775 by R. Bell, Bookseller, to which John Gill had easy access.

Though Greenfield Hall was built in 1841 during the Classic Revival architectural period, it does not hesitate to borrow its architectural charms from the earlier colonial period, incorporating some exterior and interior details from the later period. Built of pressed brick in common bond with fine mortar joints, its handsome Italianate frontispiece with full entablature, supported by bold console brackets and recessed panels in its double doors, makes a majestic entrance. The horizontal transom above the entrance with multiple rectangular muntin pattern is a hallmark of the Classic Revival style.

There is excellence and elegance in every detail – the stone window sills and cellar window heads, the marble steps and elaborate wrought iron railing, the superb treatment of the standing seam roof with dentil cornice and curved pediment dormers. Of special import are the pairs of end wall chimneys and the beautifully designed roof balustrade with its acorn posts, connecting the chimneys and reaching across the entire front and sides of the building. True to the style of the period, the date box at the conductor head, marks not only the date but the motif of a pineapple, symbol of hospitality.

Above: *The beautiful balustrade and dormers on the original standing seam tin roof of Greenfield Hall.*

68

FRONT ELEVATION.

Above: *The front elevation of the John Gill IV house, one of eight historic houses in Haddonfield included in the Historic American Buildings Survey of New Jersey, compiled and edited by the National Park Service, Department of Interior.*

Above: *Queen Anne mirror and marble-top table, 1740, were brought over from England by Elizabeth Haddon Estaugh on one of her trips. Very few marble-top tables were made then. Original 18th century Queen Anne chairs are acquisitions.*

Opposite: *The front parlor, one of the double parlors on the west side, reflects the Classic Revival style of the 1840's period in Haddonfield. Simple black marble fireplaces downstairs, gray marble in the bedrooms. Beautiful woodwork and 12 feet high five panel doors. The Queen Anne bird cage tea table was given by Mrs. Chew of Haddonfield, a descendent of the Chew family, and was brought over from England by Benjamin Chew who was secretary to William Penn, arriving on the same ship.*

Samuel Mickle House, early 1700's

345 King's Highway East

Opposite: *The original color was red which was replicated in the restoration.*

The quality of significance in American history, architecture, archeology and culture is present in districts, sites, buildings, structures and objects of state and local importance that embody the distinctive characteristics of a type, period, or method of construction.

Criteria, National Register

If this primitive early colonial structure, built by Samuel Mickle, looks out of place next to Greenfield Hall, the elegant Georgian style Gill mansion, it is because it has been moved there from 23 Ellis Street, where it was moved in 1836 from its original location next to the "Old Tavern," (the Indian King) to make way for the three John Clement brick houses which Clement built for his three daughters and which still stand at 227-229-231 King's Highway East. In 1965, the Historical Society, in order to save this oldest dwelling extant in Haddonfield from demolition, raised the funds to relocate and restore the little house. Louis H. Goettelmann, AIA, then president of the Historical Society, engineered the move and engaged in its restoration with the noted restoration architect, John Milner.

The "Hip Roof House," as it is called, though it has a gambrel roof, has an interesting history. Samuel Mickle was a descendant of the Mickle family who arrived in America as part of the Quaker migration of the late seventeenth century, settling in Newton Township, Gloucester County (now Camden County). He built the one and a half story building as his saddlery shop, on the lot where stood a brick house which he purchased from John Kaighn in 1736, according to early deeds. This was undoubtedly his home. When Samuel Mickle died in 1748, he directed in his Will that the property be put up for sale. In the Pennsylvania Gazette, September 22, 1748, the following advertisement appeared: "To be sold or let a commodious brick house, a lot with good shop and barn situate in Haddonfield, Gloucester County, the lot contains an acre and a half with near a hundred fruit trees. The situation is very convenient for a shop keeper or tradesman." The shop was the "Hip Roof House."

The Samuel Mickle building also has the distinction of being the only house remaining in Haddonfield that can be associated with Elizabeth Haddon. She bought this property in 1752 from the Samuel Mickle estate, and held it until her death in 1762 when she willed the brick residence to Sarah Lord Hopkins, the wife of her deceased nephew, Ebenezer Hopkins, who was to be her heir. She willed the other part "in tenure," presumably the little one and a half story building, to Sarah Lord's daughter, Ann. Sarah Lord may never have lived in the brick house, but used it as a rental property. The "Hip Roof House" may have been converted into a dwelling. It had two rooms downstairs and two rooms upstairs and a corner fireplace.

The exterior front portion of the house has been restored to the original vertical beaded New Jersey cedar boards, with its heavy batten door. The windows are six over six lights with small shed dormers on the front of the shingled gambrel roof, a very early eighteenth century style. The wood shed in the rear was built in 1836. The plan is to restore the interior. Because of its early construction, it is considered a significant building, one of the eight Haddonfield buildings included in the Historic American Buildings Survey.

"Hip Roof House" before restoration when it was moved to Ellis Street

"Lullworth Hall," 1886

435 King's Highway East

Opposite: *The configuration of windows in the solarium on the east side and the balcony tower are among the superb architectural features.*

In its more common forms, with all their irregularities of shapes and outlines, the Queen Anne House did constitute "a delightful insurrection" against monotony. When the concept of freedom of plan and design associated with the Queen Anne style was tamed and naturalized, it led to fresh, indigenous developments of exceptional charm.

History of Notable American Houses,
American Heritage

This most magnificent example of the Queen Anne style in Haddonfield was built in 1886 as the residence of Charles H. Mann and his family. Charles Henry Mann, born in Philadelphia July 27, 1850; died in Paris, France, August 18, 1910, came to Haddonfield in 1860 with his father William Mann, president of the Philadelphia firm of William Mann, stationers. They lived at the "Lindens," the large residence built by William Coffin Jr. in 1852, at 437 King's Highway East, which was destroyed by fire in 1892.

The young son had an excellent education at Mr. Aaron's exclusive school in Mt. Holly and Burlington College which prepared him for the important posts he held in Haddonfield as a director of the National Bank of Haddonfield upon its organization on February 16, 1889, and president of the Haddonfield Electric Light and Power Company in the same year when it was given a franchise for five years to provide electricity for the town. Not surprisingly, Lullworth Hall was the first house to have electricity. It was introduced at a dramatic event which took place at a gala party at the mansion during which the gas lamps were extinguished and electric lights turned on, much to the astonishment and applause of the guests.

Among the superb architectural features of the house is the solarium on the east side with its beautiful configuration of windows, and the great balcony tower. Photographs on the walls of the solarium show the huge room when it was furnished with charming Victorian wicker chairs, settees and plant stands. The original tin ceiling is another detail found in luxurious Victorian homes. Note also the elegant porte-cochere entrance, the double porches with beautifully designed turned posts and brackets, connected with lovely lattice work.

The interior architecture is equally luxurious. The center hall staircase is a tour de force of Victorian craftsmanship. As you ascend the stairs you are overwhelmed with the carvings, ornamentation and heavy design motifs. Upon reaching the landing you face a rare stained glass window attributed to the famous Tiffany. In the original dining room, the unique feature are the windows, with a rare treatment of convex and concave panes. The large oak fireplace mantle in this room is richly ornamented in an acanthus design, very popular in this period.

The Mann mansion was purchased by the Bancroft Training School after the fire of 1892 had dislodged them from their home at the "Lindens." The purchase was made possible by Charles Lippincott, of Philadelphia, who had been acquainted with the brilliant work of its founder, Margaret Bancroft, in educating mentally deficient "special" children. The property, then owned by William Mann, had been for rent and Charles Lippincott made a mutually advantageous offer to the school. He would settle the property upon the school for life in return for their care of his daughter.

The Bancroft School has expanded with additional buildings on the property; the original Mann mansion is now used for administrative offices, with care taken to preserve the architectural integrity of the building. A delightful restoration has been the Cottage Garden in front of the greenhouse, which also provides educational opportunities for Bancroft students. Old pictures were researched in order have some sense of the original design of the landscaped grounds.

Above: *The staircase at Lullworth Hall is a handsome example of the heavy, ornate craftsmanship of the late Victorian period.*

Above: *Lullworth Hall's elegant porte-cochere entrance leads to beautifully designed lattice-ornamented porches.*

Daniel Fortiner House, 1820

8 Roberts Avenue

Above: *Daniel Fortiner house, built in 1820, was moved to 8 Roberts Avenue from 202 Main Street (King's Highway) in 1949 where it was severely altered for commercial store use. Restored under the guidance of Herbert Leicht, restoration architect, its restoration of the original exterior and interior design continued over the years by a succession of owners. The lovely lines and proportions, the fine architectural details of the early Federal period in Haddonfield, are now readily apparent.*

Willits-Appleton House, 1836

22 Roberts Avenue

Above: *Built by Nathan Willits in 1836, and later the home for many years of Lawrence Appleton, this is one of Haddonfield's finest restorations done by Herbert Leicht, noted restoration architect, who lived here until his death in 1967. The house was moved from 428 King's Highway in 1914 to save it from demolition. Excellent Federal period architectural details. Charming small boxwood garden and landscape plan were part of the "rebirth" of this picture-book house.*

Potter Street, 1810 to 1906

King's Highway to Fowler Avenue

*A village lane, quiet and plain, is Potter Street; there
shade-trees meet o'erhead, and there the robins pair.*
James Lane Pennypacker
Haddonfield

Opposite: *Principal elements of the exterior of the
Thackara House are unaltered, the early nine over
nine pane windows on the first floor, six over six on
the second; triangular dormers and brick chimneys
at both ends. The front door is also original.*

No other street in the historic core of Haddonfield is so
little changed from its 19th century architectural origins
as Potter Street. While the earliest streets in the Historic
District yielded to 20th century construction and
inappropriate alterations, Potter Street retained its historic
picturesque charm. Potter Street was formerly a private
road, first opened to the public in 1798. It was then
named "New Long-a-Coming Road." In 1805, the first
Pottery in Haddonfield was built where No. 50 Potter
Street now stands. It was built and operated by John
Thompson, and in 1816 was bought by Richard W.
Snowden who learned the trade from Thompson.
Snowden engaged in the business until his death in 1868,
when it was taken over by his son, who died in 1883.
The business continued and flourished under his
successor, Charles Wingender, who through his
exceptional skill and capable management won wide
recognition for Wingender pottery. The business had
thrived on this street for 100 years, until 1904, when it
was moved to Lake Street. The street was then renamed
"Potter Street," as a memorial to the enterprise with
which it was so long associated.

The exception to the early streetscape is No. 15 Potter
Street. Built in 1850 by Colonel Jesse Peyton as a social
hall for gatherings and entertainment, it was named
Hendry Hall, in honor of his friend Dr. Charles H.
Hendry, the town's most notable physician. The project
was not successful and the house was later remodeled to
become, for many years, the spacious home of Samuel
Clement and his family. Sadly, before the enactment of
the Historic District Ordinance in 1971, the architectural
integrity of the 19th century house with its charming
Victorian porch and beautiful gardens was demolished.
Inappropriate, "modernized" alterations have obliterated
all that gave character and charm to the dwelling.

Each of the houses on Potter Street, now protected by
the Historic District Ordinance and listed in the National
Register, has an interesting social and architectural
history. The Thackara House, 24 Potter Street, is one of
the eight houses in Haddonfield selected for inclusion in
the Historic American Buildings Survey of New Jersey.
Plans, elevations, details and data are in the archives of
the Library of Congress. The earliest date known for this
house is 1819, from an old deed when it was sold to
William Fortner. Obviously, the house was there before
that date. This deed shows the signatures of Thomas
Redman, Jr., Joseph Porter and Samuel Brown,
Commissioners. In 1856 it was bought by Samuel
Thackara, who for years had a blacksmith shop at the
southeast corner of King's Highway and Grove Street.
Samuel was twice a widower when he bought this house,
but soon married Mary Albertson, twenty years younger
than he. Her condition of marriage was that Samuel build
a second story over the kitchen, and a pump inside, to
which he agreed. Mary lived a vigorous and independent
widow for fifty years, until 1911, when she died at the
age of 101.

The house fell into disrepair, the original Federal-style
entrance portico torn off and replaced by a Victorian
porch, interior architectural details altered. It was rescued
in 1933 by Milton Andrews, a builder and father of the
present owner, Mrs. Caravelli and her husband Ernie,
who bought the house in 1977 through the Caravelli
family. Milton Andrews removed the Victorian porch and
replicated the beautiful original portico, the design
discovered in an old photo. Through his builder's skill,
he was able to restore much of the altered and damaged
parts of the interior.

Today, the Thackara House represents one of the
loveliest dwellings built in the town during the early
Federal period.

Githens House, 1821

19-21 Potter Street

This early house and adjoining workshop present a charming picture of how our tradesmen lived and worked. Built on land purchased by Jacob Roberts, glass manufacturer, from Isaac Kay, in 1821, it was sold after the death of Roberts in 1829 to William Githens, cabinet maker and shop joiner, who plied his trade, as did his son after him, in the small workshop building, No. 21 Potter Street. In later years the workshop was jokingly referred to as the "morgue," as coffins were made here for Haddonfield citizens. William's son, Charles, was a colorful figure around town, remembered for his shock of red hair and as a talented musician on the violoncello, performing frequently in the Baptist Church.

The house eventually became the home of Mrs. Abbott S. Willits, a Quaker lady of great charm, and a gifted artist. During the "Victorian-mania" era of the late 19th century, these simple early buildings were altered and added to with Victorian appurtances and a gingerbread porch. After a few years of vacancy had befallen the buildings, they were purchased by Mr. and Mrs. Lewis W. Barton, of nearby Barton farms, who engaged Herbert R. Leicht, a leading restoration architect, to research and restore the original 1821 architectural character of the two buildings. Later, owned by Dr. Robert Bachman, the two structures were joined together to expand the living space. The work was done by another noted local restoration architect, Louis H. Goettelmann, who used all old material on the exterior and interior and matched every detail of the original buildings. Set back from the two old buildings, the addition does not detract from the early character of the Potter Street streetscape.

Above: *The Githens House and Workshop as they appeared after restoration in the 1950's by Herbert R. Leicht, whose work uncovered the original architectural integrity of the buildings*

34 Potter Street, 1810

Not only does this house send you back to the earliest times in Haddonfield, but it gives you an idea of the simple beauty that was built into the town's early houses.

This charming, modest house is one of the earliest houses built on Potter Street. The date was determined by its early construction after an analysis by the late Herbert R. Leicht, restoration architect, who in the 1960's advised the owners at that time, Harry and Edith Atkinson, on the interior restoration of the dwelling. The house is also architecturally significant because it typifies a style found in other houses of this early period located on our oldest streets.

Despite later changes and restorations, original features still remain. On the interior, the beautiful wide-width yellow pine floors, a wood that was plentiful at that time in the region; the upstairs back windows with their colonial six over six window panes, and the woodwork. The first and second floor front windows were replaced in the mid-nineteenth century with four over four panes, the "vogue" at that time, and the window openings narrowed to fit. The old standing seam tin roof is intact; the chimney is a later installation built inside the foundation for a stove in the living room. The paneled front and side doors have been replaced with doors appropriate to the period, but the rectangular, mullioned transom is original, a design used on other houses of the period, for example the 1811 Thomas Redman tenant houses on Grove Street.

When the Atkinsons modernized the kitchen in 1963, they found the old cooking fireplace but decided not to restore it as they needed the wall space. But the fireplace is another clue to the age of the house. The kitchen leads to a "pleasure garden," enclosed by a white picket fence with English boxwood bordering the old brick paths, an enchanting garden reminiscent of Williamsburg, where the Atkinsons attended many garden symposiums.

Today, the simplicity of the exterior belies the elegant decor of the interior, the achievement of Janet and Arthur Craig, present owners, whose knowledgeable taste in furnishing the house with antiques and devotion to preserving its historic character is an inspiring illustration of what treasure can be mined in these old houses.

Above: *34 Potter Street. One of the earliest houses built on Potter Street, it underwent restoration and some alteration and typifies a simple style found in other houses of the early period located on our oldest streets.*

Samuel A. Willits House, 1871

49 Grove Street

The post-Civil War climate suggested that permanency was a thing of the past, yet many Victorians clung to the ideal that a building, whether a residence or a business structure, should last, to be handed down with pride from generation to generation.
Portraits of American Architecture,
Harry Devlin

Opposite: *The three-story Second Empire style with its characteristic mansard roof and decorative dormers was the popular style of the period.*

Despite twentieth century structures of little distinction crowding the fine original nineteenth century dwellings on one of the oldest streets in Haddonfield, a discerning eye can readily see why Grove Street from King's Highway to Lake Street was included in the boundaries of the Historic District. Of the 29 structures on the street, sixteen were built from 1811 to 1880. Of these, a few have been badly altered in the years before Historic District regulations, but several have been preserved in their original state, as 31 Grove Street and the Thomas Redman tenant houses at 82-84 Grove Street, and a few have been restored, as 49 Grove Street.

This largest and most elegant of the nineteenth century houses on the street is testimony to the glories of domestic architecture this country produced in the last century, when materials were abundant, labor was cheap and craftsmanlike, and architectural styles changed with the fashion.

Samuel A. Willits built this imposing house for his bride, Abigail Bispham Evans, whose family owned the mill and mansion at Evans Pond, now Walworth Park. Samuel operated a coal and lumber business on Linden Avenue, facing Haddon Avenue, which became the Allied Coal and Lumber Company, a town landmark, until it was torn down in the 1960's, replaced by an office building.

The Willits had five children. They worshipped regularly at the monthly Meeting of Friends on Friends Avenue. Sam Willits died in 1919 and his widow continued to live alone in the house until her death in 1936 at the age of 93 years. After her death, the property was sold for the first time to Dr. Earl S. Hallinger who founded the Ear, Nose and Throat Clinic in the West Jersey Hospital where he was chief of staff.

He had an office in his home and in Camden. Dr. Hallinger died in 1957. In 1978, Dr. J. S. Biesenkamp purchased the house for a doctor's office and residence. The house had been stripped of many of the Victorian details that gave it its charm and elegance. With the supervision of the Philadelphia architectural firm, Contemporary Design, specializing in the restoration of old buildings, Dr. Biesenkamp undertook the exterior and interior restoration. The delightful gingerbread trim on the front and side porticos which had been removed were replicated from an old photo. The original outside shutters were repaired, repainted and rehung. The beautifully designed bay window on the side of the house is the focal feature of the living room. All the rooms are of impressive size. The magnificent crystal chandelier which once hung in the dining room now hangs in the room left of the entrance in what was originally the front parlor. Now one can see the Victorian grandeur of this house — reborn.

Thomas Redman Tenant Houses, 1811

80-82 Grove Street

Now authentically restored and a very charming, picturesque addition to the streetscape.
       Louis H. Goettelmann, AIA

From this early, simple rustic double house we learn a great deal about early construction in Haddonfield and the kind of housing wealthy landowners and merchants built as rental "tenant" houses, a popular means then, as now, to produce income. Built by Thomas Redman, the village apothecary and conveyancer, these tenant houses were constructed with wooden pegs, not nails. The siding is horizontal rough cut wood, no two boards alike. The old stone foundation is intact after more than 175 years, the windows still have their original six over six window sash, the simple trim, doors and plain transoms of the early nineteenth century.

The land upon which the houses are built came down from Elizabeth Haddon who acquired in 1698 large tracts of land in what we know as Haddonfield from her father John Haddon of London. Elizabeth Haddon's cousin, John Gill 1 bought three parcels of land from her in 1732, adding to the original 87 acres he had acquired in 1728. The parcel of land on what is now Grove Street descended through several owners to Thomas Redman, grandson of John Gill, who retained much of the land he had acquired from the Gill tract. In 1811, he deeded six acres, 1 rod, 31 perches, to his son, Thomas Redman, Jr. who built the tenant houses and sold them with three and three quarters acres in 1830 to William H. Richards.

Despite a succession of owners and dwindling land, insurance records show that as late as 1873 the tenant houses were "in good, tenantable condition." However, in the twentieth century these architecturally significant structures were bound for demolition by decay and were rescued in 1960 by local historians, George and Elizabeth Lyons. Their extensive renovation included installing electricity, water and sewer service, central heating and a kitchen. Until that recent time, a bake oven in the basement, a well and an outhouse were still being used. Their preservation is further insured by the inclusion of Grove Street in the Historic District.

"Boxwood Hall," 1799

John Estaugh Hopkins House
65 Haddon Avenue

Almost two centuries old, this house still keeps its strength and beauty.

Haddonfield's choicest eighteenth century dwelling is one of the few which is all original, unaltered. It is admired for its simplicity of exterior design and interior arrangement, satisfying and pleasing to the eye of a connoisseur who described it as "cool, quiet and substantially constructed, bespeaking the excellence of workmanship of an eighteenth century artisan and the good taste of its owner."

John Estaugh Hopkins built this house in 1799 on land which was part of the original land grant to Elizabeth Haddon. Having no children she willed most of her estate to her grandnephew, John Estaugh, including her residence Haddon Hall (now 201 Wood Lane) and "all of my plantation and tract of land called New Haddonfield," making him a very large landowner. Two months after his aunt's death in 1762, he married Sarah Mickle and lived in the Estaugh mansion for thirty-eight years. They had eight children, two of whom died in infancy. In 1775, during the Revolutionary War, John enlisted third class in Captain John Stokes Company, Col. Joseph Ellis' Regiment.

After the war John turned over the Estaugh mansion and estate to his eldest son James and built this beautiful house which he named Boxwood Hall, after the many boxwood plants he brought with him from the Estaugh farm. He chose the site of the house to be near the Friends Meeting House which at that time was located where the present Fire House is on Haddon Avenue, just steps away from Boxwood Hall. John and his wife were both elders and overseers of the Meeting.

It is no wonder that this early colonial house has survived the ravages of age. Every detail of Boxwood Hall's construction is recorded in documents carefully preserved by its subsequent owners. The house rides on 8 x 10 inch white oak sill, 30 feet long. Scantlings are 5 x 10 and 5 x 11 white oak, length 16 to 20 feet. The exterior is sheathed with "2,400 feet of ceder Boards Square Edged," and the foundation is made of 3,000 bricks for which Hopkins paid John and Michael Hanchman "the sum of Nineteen Dollars and one hafe of

a Dollar" on April 20, 1799. Except for the brickwork, most of the bills are calculated in pounds, shillings and pence. In 1799, U.S. money was a somewhat dubious currency. Many Haddonfield tradesmen preferred reliable English money. Even the Hanchman bill has a parenthetical note that $19.50 was equivalent to seven pounds, six shillings and threepence.

The colonial design details are worthy of note by the viewer enjoying a walking tour of the Historic District. Windows which define the character and age of the house are, on the first floor, nine over nine panes; on the second floor, six over six panes. The colonial portico is perfectly proportioned to the building and adds a fine centering element to the asymmetry of the design. The paneled entrance door is one of the loveliest in the town. It may be that the main house was added to the recessed wing with its earlier eighteenth century gambrel roof and shed dormers, one dormer strangely abutting the wall of the later colonial house. Viewed separately it is very much like the "hip roof" house, now at 345 King's Highway East, built c. 1720's. The original wood shingle roof has been maintained, as well as the massive inside chimneys.

John Estaugh Hopkins died in 1806 leaving the property to his wife Sarah. The property passed to their daughter Hannah in 1808, then to their granddaughter, Beulah Hopkins in 1838. In 1839 Beulah, at the age of 48, became the second wife of Samuel Nicholson who lived to be 92. After his death, his daughters Rebecca and Sarah continued to live at Boxwood Hall. Later it was the home of their niece Elinor and her husband William Elkinton, the last of the descendants to live at Boxwood Hall.

Friends School, 1786

47 Haddon Avenue

Friends School, built in 1786, preceded public education in Haddonfield by many years. During the first hundred years of settlement, there was no formal school in Haddonfield. John Estaugh Hopkins who built "Boxwood Hall," at 65 Haddon Avenue, gave a piece of his land for the school, which began as a one-room brick structure. The school has undergone several major additions over the past two centuries, but its colonial architectural features and Quaker simplicity have been retained.

Friends Meeting House, 1851

Friends Avenue

Friends Meeting House was the third Meeting House built by the Friends. The first was a log building built in 1721 on land deeded to Elizabeth Haddon Estaugh by her father John Haddon, located where the fire station now stands. In 1828, a new party arose within the Quaker movement, following the teachings of Elias Hicks. As a result, Haddonfield Meeting split into Orthodox and Hicksite Friends. Both groups made separate use of the same Meeting House until the Orthodox Party built the present Meeting House in 1851. The Hicksites then built their own Meeting House at Walnut and Ellis Street which was sold to Haddonfield Acme Market when the two groups were reunited in 1952. Nobody built better than the Quakers, and the Meeting Houses of the Friends are models of beautiful masonry and simple, generous proportions.

The Clement Street Houses, c. 1880's

Between Tanner and Mechanic Streets

The houses are the ultimate of simplicity. Their basic utility and economy of scale probably saved them from demolition over the course of more than one hundred years.

Charles Weiler, AIA

This charming Victorian streetscape, reminiscent of the British Mews, consists of seven small dwellings in three separate buildings, the only buildings on one-block long Clement Street, formerly known as "Parkham's Alley" until 1895. They were intended as rental cottages for workmen and transients and have continued as rental residences to this day. The date when they were built is indeterminate. They do not appear on the 1877 map of Haddonfield and they are of a design used over a thirty-year period. In 1895, Charles and Fannie Smith, owners of Smith's Livery Stables, were granted a mortgage by the Camden Safe Deposit Co. on the seven row houses which were adjacent to their livery stables. In May, 1911, Fannie Smith, now a widow, sold these houses to Benjamin Wood who lived in his beautiful family home at 209 King's Highway West. It was an investment for Ben Wood and he held the properties until 1970 when he sold them to the present owners, Albert and Mary Bauer.

Following a fire a few years ago, the exterior and interior of the cottages were carefully restored by Albert Bauer, a skilled craftsman. No architectural detail which had been lost or damaged was too obscure to require careful replacement. Constructed in traditional row house style, the three detached buildings have simple raised portico entrances, with interesting Victorian cut out brackets in a design of chariot wheel and fish pattern, taken from a pattern book available at the time. Albert Bauer's replication of these brackets which were destroyed by the fire is remarkable. Characteristic of the period are the original shutters, solid panel on the first floor, louvered on the second, and the standing seam tin roof.

The interior of each house has a front parlor, a rear kitchen with eating area; upstairs are two small bedrooms and added bath. The house at the corner of Mechanic Street has a dining room with lovely bay window. From a rear shed which was the old kitchen, the Bauers built a handsome new functional kitchen, powder room and pantry closet. They also created a Victorian ambience around the house, installing original Philadelphia Victorian street lamps in the rear parking area as part of a landscape plan. Set only one block off the King's Highway shopping area, they remain a valuable asset to the downtown neighborhood, both architecturally and historically.

Jeremiah Elfreth Houses, c. 1798

Nos. 10-12 Tanner Street

*These choice early twin houses are one of the reasons
Tanner Street was placed in the Historic District, which
will insure the preservation of their charming late
colonial character.*

Louis H. Goettelmann, AIA

These two and a half story twin brick houses, No. Ten,
now an office; No. Twelve, a shop, were built as
residences on land conveyed to Jeremiah Elfreth in 1798.
An early deed, dated 1814, records that Elfreth sold the
twin houses to Benjamin Bispham for $266.67. The
colonial style six over six pane windows, the dormers
and brick belt course above the first floor are original in
No. Ten. In No. Twelve, only the front first floor
windows have been replaced by a bulk window, an
alteration that was made before the regulations for
preservation in the Historic District Ordinance. No. Ten is
the better preserved of the two buildings, both exterior
and interior. On the interior, original architectural details,
chair rails, doors, woodwork and the beautiful fireplace
mantel in the front room have been sensitively
maintained by a succession of owners.

Tanner Street is one of the earliest streets in
Haddonfield. It is interesting to note that in a Deed of
1817, Tanner Street was called Lower Street. However, a
previous Deed, signed by Elizabeth Estaugh, exists in
which she sells for the sum of one hundred and twenty
pounds Proclamation money to Isaac Andrews, Tanner, "a
certain peace of Lott, Bounded in the manner following,
VIZ: Beginning at a corner made by the Road called
Tanners Street and the Road that leads from Burlington to
Salem and runs from thence by said Road, being ye Kings
Road," (and so forth). This Deed was for two acres of
land across Tanner Street. Elizabeth Haddon Estaugh died
in 1762 and Tanner Street was one of her early holdings.
On a portion of her Tanner Street land, Isaac Andrews, a
tanner, built a house and tannery in 1739. This house,
bearing a historical marker, is at No. 38 Tanner Street.

Above: *Nos. 10 and 12 Tanner Street, built c. 1798. These twin brick houses, now painted white, are charming examples of the early homes built on one of the oldest streets in Haddonfield.*

Estaugh Inn,
1870–1740

8 Tanner Street

Above: *Historic Estaugh Inn, built in 1740 on land owned by Elizabeth Haddon Estaugh.*
The front part was rebuilt in 1870, in Victorian style, as a residence by Isaac Middleton.
Part of the 1740 structure with original colonial details intact may be seen in rear.
Converted to commercial use in 20th century, the original four over four pane windows
on the first floor were replaced with bulk windows. Original are the second and third floor
windows, narrow wood siding, heavy double paneled entrance doors and mullioned
horizontal transom. Since 1976, the Antiques and Flower Shop of Eleanor Vail.

26-26 ¹/₂ Tanner Street

Above: *Nos. 26-26 ¹/₂ Tanner Street. Built about 1810, these two-story twin houses are two of the choice early houses which have survived on the street. All original are the wide inset chimneys, tin roof, nice cornice work, with original beaded horizontal siding, the nine over six pane windows on the first floor, six over six on the second floor, paneled shutters, six panel doors. These charming early 19th century dwellings are significant to the historic character of Tanner Street, one of the oldest streets in Haddonfield.*

Gibbs Tavern, 1777

127-129 King's Highway East

Many favorable comments have been received on what an improvement this rehabilitation has made in what was an ugly spot on our colonial style business section. It is again one of our most important and oldest historic structures.

Louis H. Goettelmann, AIA

Gibbs Tavern, built in 1777, its date inscribed in the brick facade on the west side of the building, is one of the two remaining colonial tavern buildings in Haddonfield. The other is the famous Indian King, built in 1750, now a State Museum. Severely altered on the exterior and interior in the 20th century, regarded as the "ugly duckling" of the King's Highway business district, it was the hope of the town that someday someone would purchase it for rehabilitation. The opportunity came when the building was sold in November, 1983, to Sandra and Jack Leonard, local realtor, who commissioned Louis H. Goettelmann Associates, restoration architects, to undertake the project.

The colonial building began as the private home of Edward Gibbs, a blacksmith by trade who operated a smithy at the rear of the property, elements of which were maintained intact in the rehabilitation. The first person to be granted permission to keep an inn in this building was Jacob Roberts in March, 1779. In his petition for a tavern license he stated that he was "ever ready to evince his attachment to the public weal as far as his mite extends, both in purse and person."

The Gibbs house continued as a tavern with a succession of innkeepers well into the 1830's, more than fifty years. In 1824, a stage was established between Camden and Haddonfield and the mail came regularly twice a week. Wagons brought hay which was sold to Haddonfield customers. Enoch Clement, then the Gibbs Tavern innkeeper, was the weigher, with the scales kept at the inn. The end of taverns in Haddonfield came when in 1873 the town voted against the sale of liquor. In later years, the building housed the town's post office.

In the 1920's a bulk window treatment of marble and glass extending beyond the original building line and the gutting of the entire first floor interior to accommodate a store left very little of the original structure, although the upper stories of this three and one-half story brick building had not been materially altered. As no documentation could be found of the original front facade, the rehabilitation took the form of an early colonial shop with classic cornice details and pilasters, recalling the architecture used in the period around the Revolution. The architects were careful to repeat cornice detail and moldings on the exterior to match existing details in size and form. The Victorian two over two window sash was replaced with the original colonial six over six panes. Shutters which had been removed were replaced with old shutters and hung on existing hinges. Also replaced was the wood cedar shingle roof, removing the slate whose weight had caused deflection in the bridge of the roof. All rafters in the roof and all joists in the entire building are pegged, indicating the 18th century construction. Since the old brick had been painted, it was repainted in colonial colors.

When the rehabilitation job was completed in May, 1984, Jack Leonard, the owner remarked, "The Historic District is the town's pride and joy and we feel the Gibbs house is now truly a historical treasure both to the eye and to Haddonfield's architectural heritage."

Nathan Willits House, 1836

8 King's Highway West

My first memories of the old house center around the Cattels (Senator Alexander Catell, elected 1866), who lived there when I was a child, and whose adopted daughter was my playmate. The house was always a handsome one, as it is today, and the interior appointments were very impressive, for those who lived there possessed the means and taste to keep up the place.
Memoir, Sarah R. Murray, 1929

This handsome house, one of the two historic houses of the Federal period which have survived on King's Highway West, has had the good fortune of having been lovingly cared for, its architectural integrity preserved, by a succession of owners, including the present owners, Eugene and Myra Kain. Built by Nathan Willits in 1836, a member of the prominent local Willits family, the house has been the residence of several notable owners, including Alexander G. Cattell who was elected United States Senator in 1866, and held other important posts in business and politics. President Ulysses S. Grant regarded him as one of his wisest advisers and best friends.

Another notable resident was Dr. Franklin E. Williams who moved to the Willits house in 1871 after a large and lucrative practice in Germantown, Pennsylvania, the first physician to establish homeopathy there. He retired because of ill health and moved to Haddonfield "attracted by the natural beauties of the place and its resemblance to a New England village." He continued his practice here for fourteen years at a less demanding scale, when he sold the property to James Stretch in 1917, who, though changing the use of the property to a funeral home, carefully preserved the original exterior and interior character of the building.

In a memoir written by Mrs. Sarah R. Murray in 1929 she recalls her visits to the house when the Cattells lived there in the 1860's and the years thereafter. "It is presumed that Nathan Willits lived in the house he had built until his death for people of his class did not move very often in those days. In 1853, the house was purchased by Edward Edwards of Philadelphia, a man of large means, who made many improvements to the place.

He had an English landscape gardener lay out the plan for the garden, planted most of the shrubbery and trees, and placed a very ornamental iron fence in front." A section of the beautiful iron fence remains at the rear of the property but has been removed from the front. "The garden remains as it was when Edwards' English gardener completed it. Vines galore twine around arbors and trellises attached to the rear of the house; winding box-edged paths and an English boxwood maze are the landscape plan of the formal garden." Edwards employed a local German gardener, John Yackley, to maintain the garden which was the pride of its successive owners and the town. A portion of garden remains as it was when Edwards' English gardener completed it. The English boxwood maze of the old formal garden has been beautifully maintained. The old "pavilion," with its diamond-shaped lattice, the arched grape arbor, still retain an old-world atmosphere at the rear of this property.

The dignity and simplicity of this historic Federal period building never fail to charm. The interior is also exemplary of the period with beautiful woodwork and doors. Through 155 years it has maintained its rich residential character, despite its change of use, thanks to its caring owners.

Above: *Boxwood Garden*

Above: *Original "pavilion" with diamond-shaped lattice has been well preserved.*

John W. Swinker House, 1828

18 King's Highway West

A small gem

Louis H. Goettelman, AIA

When this small house was built in 1828, it fit comfortably into the early 19th century streetscape on King's Highway West, an area just developing. Next door, where now is the 1880 Victorian mansion, was the 1820 home purchased as a residence in 1836 by John W.'s father, John A. Swinker. This home was moved to 34 Warwick Road after John W. Swinker's death. At the corner of King's Highway and Warwick Road was the David Roe house, built in 1827, and in 1836, Nathan Willits built his fine house at #8 King's Highway West. What a harmonious architectural streetscape of the Federal period in Haddonfield! But the street scene was to change in the second half of the century. Several Victorian buildings were constructed, crowding the space between the early buildings. The little John W. Swinker house was overtaken by the Victorian trend. A small side porch was added with gingerbread brackets, the two story building with a low pitched roof, documented in an old photo, was raised to two and a half stories with a steep pitched roof and a single narrow gable dormer. The added roof gutter fascia was ornamented with drop finial brackets.

The simple house built in the colonial style was gone. Its early architectural details may still be seen in the stepped window moldings similar to the 1820 Swinker house moved to 34 Warwick Road. A complete restoration of the property to its Victorian styling, which had also been altered through the years, was undertaken by the Covenant Bank which took possession of the property in 1987. The Bank took care to preserve whatever interior architectural details remained of the original building within the functional plan of the bank. In view on the second floor is further evidence of the early construction of the Swinker House—showing that all the walls were filled with brick, used as a basis for the finishing of plaster, which also added mass and retained heat. One of these walls is revealed to show this original architectural detail. The old shed in the rear was converted as part of a spacious conference room overlooking a beautiful landscaped garden.

David Roe House, 1827

32 King's Highway West

Opposite: *The handsome portico, block-paneled double doors and fan-shaped leaded glass transom create a magnificent entrance in the Federal style.*

(David Roe) One of the best and most systematic agriculturists in the neighborhood.
Prowell's History of Camden County

One of Haddonfield's finest houses of the Federal period, this residence was built by David Roe, Sr., a descendent of one of the oldest families in Gloucester County, NJ, who settled in the province of New Jersey as early as 1700. David Roe was born in 1800 and grew up on the home farm. His education was at the Woodbury Academy and was superior to that obtained by most farm sons of the time. He moved to Haddonfield in 1821, and opened a "country store" on Main Street. After his marriage in 1825 he began to purchase parcels of land along both sides of Warwick Road and Chews Landing Road, and made some ventures in farming. By 1845 his farm ownership consisted of more than 100 acres. His increased land holdings required his entire attention and he closed his business as a merchant to devote himself to scientific farming. His theory was that soil properly fertilized and cultivated made the best return, and the more liberally this theory was followed the more successful was the farmer, claiming that the best was always the most economical.

David Roe seemed to apply this theory to the home he built in 1827 at the corner of King's Highway West and Warwick Road. The very best materials and excellent design went into its construction. Despite unfortunate alterations in the twentieth century, covering the original wood siding with aluminum siding, including the window trim, replacing the beautiful wood balustrade on the front steps with ordinary wrought iron, and the block-paneled shutters with stock shutters, the David Roe house retains its historic and architectural significance. Note the handsome portico entrance, the charming ornamentation in the entablature, the great block-paneled double door with very interesting leaded fan-shape glass transom.

The windows of the two and a half story building are the original six over six panes; the bay window on the east side may have been added later but its details follow those on the front portico. The original iron fence surrounds the house and the venerable English boxwood at the side and rear of the house is a constant delight to the eye of passersby.

David Roe, Jr. inherited his father's house and farm in 1855, when he was twenty-one. After his death, the estate was disposed of at a Master's Sale at Camden Court House, May 1, 1893, dividing the land into twelve lots of varying sizes. The David Roe house with 2.87 acres was sold to William Summer Long, Roe's son-in-law, for $5,900. The Long family owned the residence into the 1940's. A successive owner, William Haven, Dr. Long's brother-in-law, made the unfortunate alteration of covering the original wood siding with aluminum siding. In August, 1975, the house was purchased by Eleanor and Ira Vail and has been their residence to this day. The Vails have a very sensitive appreciation of the historicity of their house, and have been staunch supporters of historic preservation legislation in Haddonfield which, if enacted years earlier, would have preserved all the original architectural details which were the "best" David Roe could design.

Evans House, 1890

120 King's Highway West

Opposite: The distinctive diamond-shaped, vari-colored slates of the mansard roof are dramatized by projecting bays and "eyebrow" dormers.

The Victorian Second Empire style, as typified by the Evans House, was considered modern, for it imitated the latest French building fashions.

The distinctive roof, named for the 17th century French architect, François Mansart, was extensively revived in France during the reign of Napoleon III (1852-1870), France's Second Empire.

Ralph Pendrak, AIA

The exterior and interior grandeur of this elegant example of the Victorian Empire style is owed to Ellwood Evans, farmer, inventor, entrepreneur and, in 1879, Haddonfield Commissioner, who built this house on a lot he purchased in 1890 in the area which had been known as "Brickyard Pond," since earlier times had seen a brick making enterprise nearby.

This Victorian mansion was considered large even in its day of construction. It has twenty-three rooms on three floors; six rooms over thirty feet in length. The dining room could easily seat thirty people, accommodating the Evans' frequent entertaining and the Friends Monthly Meeting which had been organized in their home.

Ellwood Evans was born in 1840 near Marlton, New Jersey. Born into a farming family, he took over his father Uriah's farm at Cropwell, so named because of its high fertility, including three hundred acres, two hundred and fifty of which were cultivated. He was a very advanced and progressive farmer. He introduced steam power, built a remarkable and successful silo, and introduced imported Jersey and Guernsey cattle. He was one of the projectors of the Philadelphia Marlton and Medford Railroad which had its terminus at Haddonfield when few others had faith in the project.

Mr. Evans lived here with his first wife Sarah, a distant cousin, and after her death, with his second wife, Anna Lockwood Cowgill. They had two sons, Joseph Ellwood and Charles Henry. Ellwood Evans died in 1916 as a result of an accident, a fall from the second story at the rear of his house. Charles took over the reins of his father's interests and lived in the house with his wife Ruth Sloan until 1976. It was purchased in 1978 by its present owners, Robert and Eleanor Hill. Charles served as Borough Commissioner of Finance for over ten years and State Assemblyman from Camden County for a two year term.

Ellwood Evans' love of wood and carving is evident throughout the house, in the chestnut woodwork, the wood having been cut and milled on the Evans farm, the

glow of its patina burnished with years of polishing; the grand staircase which ascends three floors, and of special note, the design of the double front doors, a masterpiece of the woodworker's art. The eighteen large bay windows are imported Belgium plate glass and all the windows have the original indoor louvered wood shutters.

The house we see today was altered in the 1940's when the "Colonial Revival" vogue swept away the delightful elaboration and ornamentation of many of the country's Victorian houses (see opposite page). But this house is still one of the handsomest buildings of the period in Haddonfield. The concave mansard roof rises up from deep cornices supported by brackets (not removed from sides of house), which form an ornamental bridge between the roof decoration and the trim below. The simple silhouette of the structure has been embellished with bold projecting bays on either side of the symmetrical facade, and on the east side.

The town is fortunate that the present owners, Robert, an architect, and Eleanor Hill are enthusiastic about restoring the original Victorian character of the house and hope someday to replace the architectural details lost to the "colonialization" period.

Above: *The front facade of the Evans House before it was "colonialized." The highly decorative porches were removed, the strip board ornamentation on the bays, and the charming drop brackets on the front cornice beneath the roof were thought too elaborate and were swept away in the Colonial Revival period. The brackets remain on the east side of the house as patterns for future restoration of facade planned by present owners.*

Benjamin Lippincott House, 1876

43-45 King's Highway West

During the 1870's the mansard roof in one variation or another was prevalent, if not ubiquitous.
History of Notable American Houses,
American Heritage

One of the largest and most distinguished Victorian dwellings in Haddonfield, a classic example of the finest Second Empire style to be found in South Jersey, was built by Benjamin Lippincott, a prominent farmer, born in Haddonfield in 1815, a member of the family whose origins go back to 1639 when Richard and Abigail Lippincott emigrated from Devonshire, England to the New World. The Haddonfield branch of the Lippincotts had leading roles in its history, as officers in the Revolutionary War, as first members of the Methodist Church, and in an outstanding Civil War record.

Benjamin Lippincott retired from farming in 1880 at the age of 65 and gave over the management of his property to his son Benjamin A., living the rest of his life in retirement. He died in 1892, survived by his wife Priscilla, his son and two daughters who continued to live at 43 West Main Street (King's Highway) the rest of their lives.

The superb design of this mansion with its beautiful decorative details reflects the cultivated taste, discernment and wealth of its owner. In this three-story mansion one can see the splendid characteristics of the Second Empire style. The spacious verandah across the front and side with elegant architectural details in its posts, brackets and saw-tooth ornamentation of the cornice, the "dog-ear" design of the architraves above the doors and the two over two pane windows, the mansard roof with graceful "eyebrow" dormers.

The exterior and interior doors are magnificent for their height and thickness, constructed of solid oak, three to four inches thick. The present owners, Arlene and Mario Iavicoli, who purchased the Lippincott home in 1980, have restored the original beauty of the interior four-paneled doors. Second Empire style depended heavily on ornament. This can also be seen in the iron fencing that fronts the property. Mounted on a fine brick base in a beautiful design with brick entrance pillars capped by bold moldings and a classic urn finial, the fence makes a statement of architectural excellence that prepares one for the superior quality of the house.

The Lippincott house has been used as part professional offices and part residence since it was purchased by George L. Snell, a dentist, in 1943. Its exterior architectural integrity, and many of its beautiful interior rooms including the grand ballroom on the second floor, have been preserved and continue to represent a great period in the architectural history of Haddonfield.

Samuel K. Wilkins Houses, 1877

51-53 King's Highway West

Opposite: *The third floor bays with elaborate U-shaped window hoods on rounded triple window shapes were striking style-setters in Haddonfield.*

The quality of the post Civil War "High Victorian" is best described by its habit of borrowing styles, as "picturesque eclecticism."

These twin mansions are a masterpiece of Victorian architecture and unaltered represent one of the most exuberant periods in the architectural history of Haddonfield. Among those with great amounts of money to spend, a passion for building large and impressive houses in the "Gilded Age," did not by-pass this Quaker town. One of these men of wealth was Samuel K. Wilkins, a successful wholesale dry goods merchant in Philadelphia who prospered during the Civil War through large government contracts.

Samuel Wilkins was born in Woodbury, New Jersey in 1820, but in his childhood moved with his family to Haddonfield, where they lived in a house on "Main Street," built in 1800 by Joseph Collins. The house was later demolished for a gas station. Samuel married Emma Fortiner in 1854 and took his bride to his father's house. His children, Ellen Jane and Anna Kain, were born in 1855 and '57. His wife died in 1859, leaving the two baby girls, cared for by "Aunt Sue," his half-sister. The two girls grew up with all the advantages of wealth, the finest education and trips abroad. His daughter Ellen married William Thomas Barber on October 4, 1877, and that year her father built Nos. 51 and 53 King's Highway West, then named "Main Street." From all accounts, when it was built, it was considered the "model of the latest and best both in plan and construction." That year his newly married daughter moved into No. 53 and the next fall Samuel Wilkins, his other daughter Anna, and Aunt Sue moved into the new home at No. 51. The first macadamized road in Haddonfield was laid in front of these houses and was contracted for by Samuel Wilkins.

Note the exceptional architectural detailing of these houses. Constructed in the Second Empire or Mansard style which has its origins in Parisian architecture, its distinguishing feature is the steep, curved line of the double sloped mansard roof. The size and shape of the windows are also significant. Tall first-floor windows and heavily ornamented arched window heads add surface richness to the symmetrical lines that usually characterize this style. Borrowing from the popular Italianate and related Second Empire styles, there rose a profusion of elaborate window crowns. In these styles, for the first time, arched and curved window tops became a common feature. In the Wilkins houses we see this expression at its most elegant in the third floor bays with their elaborate U-shaped window hoods on rounded triple window shapes. It was in the Italianate and Second Empire styles that paired and triple windows first gained popularity. Also borrowing from the contemporaneous Italianate style are the intricately carved support brackets, and supporting columns of the porch.

The interior of No. 53 is a superlative architectural experience. From the grandly paneled front door with its exquisite stained glass transom one enters rooms with beautiful cornices, window trim and paneling under the windows, original indoor shutters, and magnificent eight panel, twelve feet high doors between rooms. Dr. Mario Gebbia who now owns the property and continues its decades-long use as a medical office, has brought this magnificent house up to its pristine origins. The Finley family still occupy No. 51, for 35 years the medical office of the late Dr. John Finley.

Above: *Elaborate porch bracket detail*

Above: *Curved window tops and ornamentation in mansard roof dormer windows.*

Willis-Thomas House, c. 1856

109 King's Highway West

The Italianate style could be as picturesque as the Gothic or as restrained as the classical.
William J. Gallo, AIA

This three-story frame house is a fine example of the early period of Italianate architecture, 1840-1860. It reduces the style to its simplest elements of square house, low pyramidal roof, bracketed eaves and cupola or lantern. What is striking to the viewer is the gesture of the composition which is so tranquil and at peace with itself and its surroundings.

Perhaps the influence of the picturesque movement is at work here. The residence is set far back from the street so one can appreciate the composition in space rather than as space. Notice how the proportional relationship between the length of the porch and the square of the elevation imply the harmonic principles prevalent in the works of Alberti and Palladio. One can almost graphically project the length of the porch extension by using the diagonal of the square elevation as the radius of an arc swung down to the first floor. The entrance portico and balustrade above were added at the turn of the century but do not impair the fine proportion of the building, but rather add to its elegance.

Of course, the most striking feature is the Tuscan influence created in the imposing lantern or "belvedere." This form, square in shape and fenestrated on all four sides is the epitome of the composition. This superb architectural element encases a fifteen square feet room.

Research has not indicated who built this important structure but the record shows it was described as "A first class building, the materials of the best to be procured." It is known that Benjamin B. Willis purchased the house about 1866 as his residence and sold it in 1877 to Benjamin B. Thomas. In the 20th century it became the medical office of Dr. Andrew Jannett and was converted into apartments. It was recently purchased by Dr. Ronald Clark who is enthusiastic about restoring the magnificent interior of this premier home on King's Highway West.

The Wood House, 1870

209 King's Highway West

Opposite: *Characteristic of the Second Empire style of the 1870's are the mansard roof, bracketed porch frieze and extended porch with decorative detailing in its supporting columns.*

People sat on their front porches in these days. The road had no surfacing, not even gravel and in dry weather when an occasional wagon did come along the prevailing south wind would blow dust in, much to the displeasure of those on the porches.

Ben Wood, Memoir, 1975

One of the few houses built in this period that was not altered and thus presents the original architectural integrity, this fine Victorian house and its charming accessory buildings were built in 1870 by John F. Hillman, descendent of John Hillman who came to America in 1697 and settled in Gloucester Township. His father, Samuel S. Hillman, lived in the house next door at 203 King's Highway West. John F. was a member of the firm of Wanamaker and Brown of Philadelphia and built his house in Haddonfield, as did his father, as a "summer" home, with an exceptional plan to utilize light. The northern side has no windows; all the major rooms are on the southwest side with long four over four pane windows in the two first floor bays – the parlor and the living room, and on the second floor, filling the rooms with light and airiness.

In 1884, the house was purchased by Jehu Wood, son of Isaac Wood, who built the historic mansion in 1842 at 201 Wood Lane. When the Wood family moved here, their son Benjamin was three years old and he continued to make this his home for his entire life. Ben Wood, as he was known, died in 1976 at the age of ninety-five.

Ben Wood recalls in a memoir written in 1975 that when his family moved to this house it had "all the latest conveniences. Most houses in the 80's and early 90's were lighted by oil lamps and candles, but our house was lighted by gas. There was a tank buried in the yard into which gasoline shipped from Philadelphia in large barrels was emptied into the tank...about one tank every three months." According to Ben Wood, his house was the second in the town to be electrified; Lullworth Hall, the Mann mansion on Hopkins Lane, was the first. The house was built with the latest central heating, the black marble fireplace mantels were just for "show." Under the meticulous eye of its owner the barn could have been an exhibition building with every tool polished and in its proper place. To this day, the small garden has a quaint charm.

Joseph F. Kay House, 1868

70 Linden Avenue

It (the Italianate style) speaks of the inhabitant as a man of wealth, who wishes in a quiet way to enjoy his wealth. It speaks of him as a person of educated and refined tastes, who can appreciate the beautiful both in art and nature.

> Samuel Sloan,
> "The Model Architect," 1852

Such a man was Joseph F. Kay, born 1825, died 1894, a prominent member of the Haddonfield community and descendent of one of the oldest and most respected families and landowners in West Jersey. He was one of the first commissioners when the borough was incorporated in 1875. Kay built one of the most aristocratic houses in nineteenth century Haddonfield on land purchased from Samuel K. Wilkins on West Main Street (King's Highway), when there was only his grand new house and his brother Isaac M. Kay's mansion, built in 1860, on that part of Main Street. In that undeveloped setting, the house was truly a "country villa," as the Italianate style house was meant to be. The same Samuel Wilkins built his Second Empire style twin mansions at Nos. 51-53 Main Street nine years later, in 1877. So one can see the development of the nineteenth century streetscape of elegant mansion-size houses on the recently opened King's Highway, west of the railroad.

Unfortunately, this streetscape was broken up when in 1900 the Kay mansion was moved from Main Street in order to open up Linden Avenue, cut through by the West Haddonfield Land Company. In this development, the Joseph Kay house was relocated at the corner of the new Linden Avenue and Euclid Avenue, probably saved because of its association with a prominent citizen. The move accounts for the out-of-character location of the Kay house among the twentieth century houses on the first block of Linden Avenue.

Through a succession of owners in the twentieth century, the great house was badly altered, but through the remarkable exterior and interior restoration by its present owners, Lee Albright and her husband, Gerard Haubrich, the house, in their words, was "reborn." The aluminum siding was removed, the altered porches restored, the missing brackets and other architectural details, including the characteristic cupola, were replaced. The exterior restoration of the building was well documented by early photos showing the house before it was moved to Linden Avenue. They show a three story wood frame house with eyebrow windows on the third floor and four over four pane double hung sash windows on the first and second floor.

Characteristic of the Italianate style is the low pitch roof, the wide projecting eaves with prominent bracketed cornice, the double doors with ornamented glass panels. The striking feature is the elaborate bracketed center front portico, topped by a bay window on the second floor. The corner supports of the porch have three posts and the restored side porch has two posts connected by a balustrade. Decorative small details add to the picturesque quality of the house—the drop finials on the cornice at the end of the brackets, the paneled corner boards, details brought out by the contrasting paint scheme.

Above: *Ornate ceiling medallion and ornamented ceiling and cornice moldings are lavish Victorian expressions. Chandelier is an 1848 reproduction.*

Opposite: *Reception Room of the 1868 Kay house captures the character of an authentic Victorian parlor. White marble fireplace was a decoration, not for burning.*

John A. Swinker House, c. 1820

34 Warwick Road
(moved from 20 King's Highway West)

Although architectural styles succeeded one another over the years, the basic constructional methods of the frame house remained unchanged for more than two centuries. Strong and durable oak gave the colonists their principal framing method.

This charming small dwelling, built in the first quarter of the nineteenth century bears a historical marker, "John A. Swinker," but Swinker did not build the house. Earliest records show that in 1825 this building was sold to Benjamin B. Cooper by William F. Griffith, so the house was in existence before that date. John Swinker bought the house and lot from the Cooper estate in 1836 for $502. By 1866, he insured the dwelling for $1,650.

Swinker came to Haddonfield from Bucks County, Pa., and learned stone masonry from Silas Willis, whose daughter he married in 1826. The house was situated where 20 King's Highway West is today, and after his death on July 2, 1880, having been his home for forty-four years, the property was sold and moved to 34 Warwick Road to make way for the present grander Victorian house built by Paul A. Davis on the Swinker lot. The move probably saved another early house from demolition but it unfortunately located the Swinker house out of context with the Warwick Road streetscape which was developed in the Victorian architectural period of the 1850's.

Designed in the center hall colonial style, this two-story, one hundred and seventy-one year old frame dwelling happily retains its original architectural features and illustrates the good craftsmanship, the knowledge of design, construction and proportion, of our early builders. The simple two-column portico, the entry door and rectangular divided lights transom, the two six over six pane windows that flank both sides of the doorway, the three nine over six pane windows on the second floor, the two small four over four round top windows, centered on the gable ends in the attic, are the hallmarks of early period design. Also typical are the "A" roof dormers with simplified dormer trim. The only ornamental details on the house are the stepped wood moldings around the windows, yet the pleasing character of the house is in its unornamented simplicity.

The Swinker house was beautifully restored in the 1970's by a previous owner, with a new kitchen and "family room," the focal point of which is a wall of old brick and a wood burning fireplace. The house has charmed hundreds of visitors on the Preservation Society's Historic House Tour.

Garrett-Raybold House, 1859

120 Warwick Road

Opposite: The round white picket fence was erected by the Aikens, the design appropriate to the period of the house and the character of the original fence.

The broad verandah encircling the house is a graceful and convenient, though expensive, appendage. It would be more highly appreciated in a warmer climate than this, but even here our hot summers make it grateful.
Sloan's Victorian Buildings, 1852

When young Joseph Garrett, age 27, and his wife, Matilda, age 25, built this "country house" on Mansion Avenue, as Warwick Road was then named, the undeveloped land all around them, as far as the eye could see, did indeed seem like deep country, a setting in which the "Italianate Villa" style was meant to be. It was a style which dominated American architecture in the northeast and midwest from 1850 to 1880, a style born in England as part of the desire of architects to turn their backs on classical and formal architectural organizations, a style commonly referred to as the "picturesque movement."

In Haddonfield, this particular home is one of the finest examples of the centered gable Italianate substyle. Not only does it contain the true-to-style details, but exhibits two unique characteristics that set it apart from the typical Italianate residence. Note the center gable intersecting the low pitch roof. See how the front wall extends into the gable and is highlighted by the pairing of the full arched windows. This pairing of form is characteristically carried forth in the large eave brackets of the cornice. The verandah wraps around the south side of the house, its ceiling supported by remarkable curved beams. The window proportions are another feature of interest. They are based upon the 8-5-3 vertical ratio, the height changing from the first level tall, to-the-floor windows to the small attic windows. This system is the basis for a system of harmonic proportion which shows up throughout the history of architecture from the Greeks to Le Corbusier.

The house also had the distinction of being shared by George A. Raybold, the first stationed Methodist minister in Haddonfield (1843) and a notable historian, with his wife and daughter, both named Mary. The Garretts had two daughters. In 1870, Helen was twelve years old and Virginia five. Helen was considered a beauty and a fashion plate when she grew up and married; "Virgie" remained a spinster and was the last to survive and live in the old mansion. When she died in the 1930's, there was still no electricity in the house. She willed the house to her neighbors, the Sharpleys, who had befriended her, and who modernized the house with two tile bathrooms and central heating. In 1955, Joan and James Aiken purchased the house with its original one-acre lot, from the Sharpleys, extended the small front parlor and created a window wall leading out to a brick terrace and planned garden, recreating the ambience of a "country villa."

Above: *1875 photo shows wrap around porch – a distinctive feature preserved to this day.*

Perkins-Hodgson House, 1852

132 Warwick Road

"This porch and its detailing attempt to transport the grandeur of southern antibellum architecture to the conservative northeast. One feels as if the lacy cut out brackets and columns were made of cast iron...at a fleeting glance we could be in New Orleans."
William Gallo, AIA

One of the largest and most beautiful Victorian dwellings in Haddonfield, with its two and one half acres of lawns, gardens and old trees, this Italianate-style mansion was built by Joel S. Perkins, a Philadelphia leather merchant. Perkins and his wife Lucy (Bailey) had many children, most of whom died young. After Perkins' death in 1907, the property was inherited by one of the remaining sons, Samuel S. Perkins, who died in 1935.

This elegant house on Mansion Avenue, as Warwick Road was then named for its streetscape in the 19th century of grand houses, some still standing, became the private residence of Clara and William W. Hodgson, a salesman with the Phoenix Paint Co. in Philadelphia, until 1952 when it was purchased by the Presbyterian Homes of South Jersey.

The house as we see it today has retained its essential architectural integrity and residential character, despite alterations such as the aluminum siding, the covering of the original windowed cupola with siding and the removal of the bold brackets under the roof matching those on the porch fascia.

Characteristics of this style are the beautiful, symmetrical proportions of the building, the tall narrow windows on the first floor, the small attic or "eye" windows on the third floor, the low pitched roof and wide overhanging eaves.

Uncharacteristically, the house overwhelms the viewer with its superb wraparound porch, the elaborate porch brackets and columns reminiscent of Southern antebellum design. As a matter of fact, its architectural source was found in a book of designs by Samuel Sloan, the noted mid-and late 19th century architect who designed several southern villas, as well as several remarkable residences in Haddonfield.

As you enter this house, note the double entrance door with its distinctive cross design raised panels, the great staircase in its wide center hall. There is a mother of pearl plug or cap at the top of the newel post, which it is rumored, covers a cavity in which the deed of the house is stored. Supposedly, when the mortgage was paid off on the house, the deed was sealed in the newel posts, using these fancy plugs.

Typical of the period, there are two parlors, a small one where the family sat, now the music room; the large parlor to the right of the hall used only for weddings, funerals and when the minister called. Handsome white marble fireplace mantels, ceiling decoration in the large parlor are only a few of the interior embellishments. The library to the rear is part of the original house. The large dining room and colonial-style brick building, added in the 1950's, provide needed facilities but these do not visually intrude on the architectural beauty of the original residence.

Frederick Sutton House, 1886

212 Warwick Road

"One of the finest examples of "Queen Anne" Victorian architecture in Haddonfield."
Louis H. Goettelmann, AIA

Opposite: *The house is painted in rich Victorian colors, selected by Dr. Roger Moss, noted author of "Victorian Exterior Decoration."*

This mansion-size, three-story frame dwelling sits back from the road on two acres of landscaped land in the historic core of the town. Its design of delightful decorative gables, dormers, bays and porches is the work of its second owner, Frederick Sutton, a wealthy Philadelphia coffee merchant, a native of County Suffolk, England, educated in private schools in Cambridgeshire, who emigrated to Philadelphia in 1870, and moved to Haddonfield in 1877. He became an important figure in the town and served as Director and Treasurer of the Electric Light Company of Haddonfield, and a Director of the Haddonfield Mutual Building and Loan Association.

In 1879 he purchased a residence at this location from John Yackley, a local German gardener, who built his house in 1871 and used his side yard as a nursery for a landscaping business. An old photo shows a modest two-story house devoid of the many beautiful and elegant architectural features we see today which were added by Sutton when he took possession of the house in 1886. The Yackley house had a cedar shingle roof; Sutton's house has a rich vari-design slate roof. The old house had no fireplaces; Sutton's house has two chimneys and three magnificent fireplaces on the first floor.

Queen Anne Victorian homes are somewhat a contradiction in terms. The style had little to do with Queen Anne for it was a form of Renaissance architecture that was in vogue during her reign (1707-1714). The Queen Anne style as we know it derives its form from the medieval models of Elizabethan England, a period existing from 1880 to 1910.

The Frederick Sutton house is a fine example of the overlapping of the two major styles of the Queen Anne period. Its general form is commonly referred to as "cross gabled roof with spindlework detailing." Of dramatic import is the true-to-style delicately turned porch balusters and cut out brackets.

At the rear of the property is the most architecturally interesting original Carriage House in the town. The two and one-half story frame building, as large as a small house, with cupola, is designed with the same details as the house, the stable doors reset back of large arches, its vergeboards ornamented and cut in the style of the period, and the wall surfaces of wood shingles, not only ornamented in scallop and other forms but set in a most unusual and decorative pattern.

During the 1930's Depression the house was converted to three apartments with disastrous removal of original paneled doors, center hall staircase, cornices and other priceless details. In 1980, the Philip Benders bought and restored the main house and the carriage house. Converted back to a single family dwelling, the partitions were removed, the lost or removed architectural details faithfully replicated or discovered in the basement and restored. The fireplaces had been plastered and painted over. Kathy Bender laboriously restored them, revealing exquisite European tiles as facing and hearth. The present owners, the Tassinis, have restored the beautiful design details of the porches, documented in an old photo.

The viewer will be rewarded to explore and digest for himself the many architectural treasures of this house, a "symphony of details," as described by local architect, William Gallo, including the original iron fence with its charming rosette design which encloses the entire front of the property.

FREDERICK SUTTON HOUSE

Above: *All the gables have heavy brackets, an 18 inch overhang, with ornamented scalloped shingles set in designs on each side of the windows in the gables. The ridge pole is ornamented metal with fish tails and finials on the corners. The double-hung windows, its large panes of glass surrounded by smaller square panes, some of stained glass, are reminiscent of the medieval.*

Above: *Porch details restored–balusters and columns are beautiful examples of knob-like beads within the body of the woodwork. Charming porch roof cornice design with unusual drop knobs and corner cut out brackets. Note ninety degree lattice below the porch.*

Above: *Restored—one of the three 19th century English style fireplaces which had been plastered and painted over, revealing beautiful European tiles. Mantle design is repeated in ceiling medallion. This one is in the parlor-library.*

Above: *Victorian elegance is embodied in every detail of the dining room. The magnificent Irish crystal chandelier, woodwork and wide molded cornice, the paneling under the long bay windows, the fireplace tiles (not seen in photo) are scenes of houses, churches, villages and landscapes. The ceiling medallion design is appropriately raised fruits and flowers.*

Washington Avenue, 1873 to 1910

The special charm of the old part of tree-lined
Washington Avenue, from Lincoln to Jefferson Avenues, is
the picture it presents of a significant and distinguishable
entity in Haddonfield's architectural history, though many
of the houses may lack individual distinction. Here on
one street, one may see the delightful diversity of styles
of the late Victorian period to the turn-of-the century.
Here are excellent examples of "Stick-Style" Victorian,
like the 1873 mansions at Nos. 127 and 200, designed by
famous architect Samuel Sloan, the first to be built on the
street; the delightful Carpenter Gothic style, at No. 114;
the elegant Second Empire style with its mansard roof, at
No. 121; and the turreted Queen Anne beauty at No. 235.
Great houses with wonderful wraparound porches, like
No. 412, mingle with the ubiquitous four-square type. As
we cross the threshold of the twentieth century, we
encounter a stone Tudor-style house at 500 Washington
Avenue, marking the beginning of farm land which
continued all the way to Tavistock.

Contractor and builder of many of the Washington
Avenue houses in the period between 1885 and 1900 was
William S. Capern whose promotion brochure claimed
"The buildings shown herein were placed in my hands
for construction by some of the leading architects." No
architects' names were given. "The buildings shown
herein" are on Washington, Linden and West End
Avenues. Capern homes stand today as monuments to his
claim that his "modern habitations are models of the
advancement effected in architectural designing and the
structural art; embracing all the latest up-to-date
provisions for comfort, health and convenience." They
were certainly built to last and have added an important
dimension to Haddonfield's architectural heritage.

Samuel Sloan "Stick-Style" House, 1873

200 Washington Avenue

It was in the suburban house that Sloan felt Americans had made their biggest step toward what he called our "Naissent Style of architecture."
                    Samuel Sloan, "The Model Architect"

The most illustrious private residence of the late nineteenth century period in Haddonfield is this most elaborately decorated "stick style" house designed by Samuel Sloan, one of the most active and widely known architects during the third quarter of the nineteenth century. He had become one of the most popular architects in Philadelphia. His clients included prominent members of Philadelphia's commercial aristocracy - the Biddles, Clothiers, Parrishes and Whartons.

It was this renown that caused William Massey, a wealthy Philadelphian and president of the Camden and Atlantic Railroad, to commission Sloan to design three houses in Haddonfield — 200 Washington Avenue, 127 Washington Avenue, and 141 Warwick Road. He also chose the master builder and well loved resident of Haddonfield, William Coffin Shinn, who built several of the beautiful mansions in the town.

William Massey built these houses as an investment, as there is no record that he ever lived in any one of them, though the one at 200 Washington Avenue remained the property of the Massey family until 1913, when it was sold to Henrietta and Isaac Collins, descendant of the Collins family, one of the founding families of the region.

External features of the three houses form a distinct group and no other houses in the area, or in any other part of Haddonfield, go as far as these three in the decorative and expressive use of weatherboarding. Significant is the fact that these three Haddonfield houses represent Sloan's only known attempt at using the "stick style," and that the Haddonfield Sloan houses are thought to be the latest known examples of Sloan's suburban residential architecture. The term "stick style" was not applied until the twentieth century.

The house at 200 Washington Avenue is the only one of the three with the original iron cresting on the roof of the bay and second floor front balcony. The house is symmetrically planned with a projecting dormer window in the center of the third story and central windows of the second story connecting it to the roof of the front porch. The elegant bay on the south side with its ornate cresting repeats the slate roof design of the porch, and provides lovely light and architectural interest to the dining room. Doorways were always a splendid feature of the nineteenth century home. Here the exquisite fluted leaded glass of the front door and transom was made in Bristol, England, the door leading into a charming vestibule and an inside door duplicating the entrance door.

The choice of this elaborate style of architecture seems somewhat daring in a town as architecturally conservative as Haddonfield. When they were built, they were among the most elaborately decorated houses in the town and were certainly the only examples of their kind. The two houses on Washington Avenue were the first to be built on that street and set the standard for set back and the size and scale of the houses in that section of Haddonfield.

The house at 200 Washington Avenue remained in the Collins family until 1966. In 1967, it was purchased by William and Mary Blake who restored the interior from a multi-family dwelling, a conversion of the 1940's, to the original single family home. They also succeeded in preventing the subdivision of the property. They researched and painted the house in the original colors — topaz, raisin and Indian Red — and restored the charming old log summer house in the Victorian garden.

Above: *Keyhole design, accented in contrasting colors, appears on all three local Sloan houses, a favorite detail of the architect.*

Above: *Original fireplace mantle is ornamented with English egg and dart design and decorative end brackets. Above, a 1720 portrait of an Irish noble child. The chandelier is Czechoslovakia crystal and silver, a family piece.*

Scovel House, 1892

412 Washington Avenue

We love the porch and use it all the time. Sitting on the porch you feel how Victorians lived, how they built for spacious, gracious living.
        Mayor John J. Tarditi, Jr.

This fine example of a Washington Avenue house is distinguished by its "broad verandah encircling the house," an architectural feature favored by Samuel Sloan, popular Victorian architect, in his book, "The Model Architect," published in 1852. He wrote it was an expensive appendage but graceful and convenient. The "wraparound" porch, as it came to be called, is seen in the more elegant and "expensive" Victorian houses in Haddonfield. It was certainly a mark of "status." The Scovel house was built by Henry S. Scovel, a member of the long line of eminent lawyers in Camden County. His son, Edwin G. Scovel inherited the house and lived there for many years. In 1975, it was purchased by Barbara and John Tarditi, who later became Mayor of Haddonfield.

The porch has graceful turned posts and a refined balustrade; to the right on the front facade is a beautiful and unusual oval stained glass window. The bold dormers on the original fish-scale slate roofs, the front and side gables with their small attic windows, and the pronounced bay window on the second floor are fine Victorian details. The Scovel house is one of the few remaining in Haddonfield with its original roof cresting. This was a custom-made house for a family of culture and taste and remains a rich legacy of nineteenth century architecture, and a testimony to its preservation by the present owners.

Carpenter Gothic, Restored, 1885

115 Lincoln Avenue

The timely invention of the scroll saw, or jigsaw, and the widespread availability of wood also produced that delightful national adaptation (of the Gothic Revival style) known as Carpenter Gothic.
        "What Style Is It?" — Preservation Press,
        National Trust for Historic Preservation

The picturesque country cottages known as Carpenter Gothic popularized by Andrew Jackson Downing, pioneer landscape architect and arbiter of midcentury taste, in his widely distributed books of plans for homes and cottages, dotted the countryside in the 1840's and 1850's and continued to be built in some areas long after the Civil War. In Haddonfield, many of these delightful country cottages enrich the streetscape in the old part of the town. This house on Lincoln Avenue, now restored, is one of the finest representations of the Carpenter Gothic style.

The Gothic Revival period of the late eighteenth and nineteenth centuries had its antecedents in England's romantic movement. This period was ablaze with passion, almost religious at times, portraying in built form symbols of architecture adapted for local materials and technology.

Carpenter Gothic houses were countrified versions of their European counterparts, embellished with local wood ornamentation worked with the new tools of the time, the circular saw and jig saw. The house at 115 Lincoln is an excellent example of the asymmetrical subtype which allowed flexibility in arrangement of rooms and created picturesque external silhouettes. Typical of its period, it displays two over two paned windows, a wall surface extending into the gable end, corbelled top chimney, double entry door, and an exceptionally charming design in its bracketed porch columns. These were restored by the present owners, Robert and Sandra Kugler, replicating the design they found in an old photo, and replacing the inappropriate wrought iron columns which had been added later.

Of particular interest is the grandly proportioned decorative gable trim or "vergeboard" on the main gable. This distinctive design utilizes a flatended arch crossbracing and decorative finial, a small scale model repeated on the small gable dormer.

Interior architectural details belie the modesty of this house, which may have been built for a tradesman, a prosperous segment of the population after the Civil War. The elegant six-panel doors between rooms, the beautifully ornamented and painted tin cornice in the parlor, the black faux marble fireplace mantel with artistic painted tracery, all have been sensitively restored by the present owners.

A charming addition to the house, seen from the street, is a Victorian pergola which leads to a new "outdoor living room" deck and garden. The design of the pergola was copied from the nineteenth century one in the garden of the Aspden-Champion-Blackwood historic house at 254 King's Highway East.

Pattern Book House, c. 1870

34 Centre Street

The pattern book houses of the more successful architect-publishers are notable for the quality of their design and workmanship; these houses frequently are featured in preservation magazines today — and usually are not identified as mail-order houses.
                    Old House Journal, December, 1980

One of the finest restorations in Haddonfield, this charming Victorian home combines the true freshness and frivolity of the late nineteenth century period. By combining a stucco exterior with carefully crafted wood detailing, an almost eclectic character is achieved. Note the Gothic gable, steeply pitched, capped by ridge poles and finials. These are juxtaposed with the dominant feature of the two-story bay with paneled frames below the characteristic Victorian two over two paned windows and cut out porch brackets. The entire composition of this pattern book house is a prime example of the quality of design and workmanship that can be achieved in the "mail-order house."

The restoration of this home is the work of previous owner, Patricia Driscoll, daughter of the late Governor Alfred Driscoll, and was overseen by local architect, Gordon Nilsen. An enclosed porch was removed and the original design open porch rebuilt. The lost lacy brackets were reproduced, copying those on nearby houses of the same period. The asbestos shingle siding under the bay windows was removed only to discover the fine original paneling.

The entire facade of the building was refurbished, restoring the original coarse grained stucco which had been scored with lines to simulate masonry joints. A new kitchen–dining-room–family room, "all-purpose" room, was added in the rear along with an "outdoor living" deck and a planned, landscaped garden — a "house with a view" created in the center of the town screening out parking lots and commercial properties.

Pat Driscoll sings praises to the Victorian house. She feels no other period has the potential for light in the rooms with its tall first floor windows and three-sided bay windows, "yet you're not living in a fishbowl." Builders of Victorian houses knew about cross-ventilation and high ceilings to keep rooms wonderfully cool and provide generosity of space.

"Steamboat Victorian," c. 1810-1870

57 Chestnut Street

"A fine example of the execution of a style into the epitome of a national folk genre."
William Gallo, AIA

On the surface this town "charmer" would seem to be a treasured example of the two-story "side gabled" folk Victorian style, typically circa 1870-1910. However, upon close examination it could be deduced that the final architectural statement evolved over three quarters of a century. Mentally remove the delightful decorative frieze around the porch and cornice and note the clapboard joint at the intersection of the gable form and the flat roof addition to the rear. What remains is probably the original structure thought to be built as servants' quarters or for hired hands working on the old Shivers farm, a wonderful example of the "vernacular style" of a simple home constructed during the period of 1810-1825.

Since "Folk Victorian" derives its design style by adapting Queen Anne or Italianate detailing to the new machine technology of the time, this home was "Victorianized" when the rear additions to the house were made. Note the Queen Anne turned spindle porch columns. The porch and roof detailing is shown in Samuel Sloan's Italian villa designs. Another stunning detail characteristic of folk Victorian is the center gable dormer and Gothic Revival pointed window on the south side of the third story. When viewed in its totality this playful, sometimes referred to as "Steamboat Victorian" residence is a fine example of the execution of a style into the epitome of a national folk genre.

At the rear of the property is the original two-story barn and carriage house, one of the few remaining and intact, a tribute to the succession of owners who could have but would not destroy this relic of this once farming community.

Bond-Wescott House, 1872

43 Chestnut Street

In those earlier houses, however freely they were designed, some deference was usually paid to a dominant theme—first the Greek, then the Gothic, and so on. Immediately following the war such themes and others of often dubious origin were as like as not combined in a single structure of no describable "style," unless it be called eclectic.

History of Notable American Houses,
American Heritage

This handsome, three-story, masonry-stucco house stands out for its classic simplicity in a streetscape and neighborhood of Victorian dwellings with all the exuberance of the late nineteenth century period. Built by Elizabeth and Simeon Bond, a maker of boots and shoes, on a lot bought on April 9, 1872 from David and Phebe Middleton, it strives for the refinement of the Classic Revival period with restrained Victorian elaboration. It is also a house obviously built by a man of means, perhaps one of the newly rich merchant class that rose after the Civil War, "with great amounts of money to spend, a passion for building large and imposing houses whose costs reached far beyond the bounds of prudence." This may explain why the house was sold at public auction in 1880 to Catherine Burroughs.

Historical distinction marked the house when in 1883 it became the home of John and Frances Wescott. John was admitted to the New Jersey bar in 1879, and was later appointed Judge of the Court of Common Pleas, a position he filled with notable ability. He was deeply interested in politics and was a candidate of the Democratic Party, once as a nominee for the State Senate in 1884, and in 1886 was made the unanimous choice of his party as a candidate for Congress in the First Congressional District. He was bestowed the honor of nominating Woodrow Wilson at the Democratic Convention of 1912, in Baltimore.

Judge Wescott's son, Ralph, a lawyer and Walt Whitman scholar, served as Register of Deeds in Camden County for many years. Marion Sturgis-Jones, his wife, a distinguished writer, published several books, and their son Roger, a Rhodes scholar, is on the faculty of Drew University.

The most prominent architectural feature of this house is the grand front portico with its double square columns repeated against the facade of the house on either side of the beautiful doorway. The entablature of the portico is in bold scale befitting the heavy columns. The rectangular transom with four lights divided by three muntins is a Classic Revival feature, but the cut out brackets on the roof cornice are distinctly Victorian, as are the one over one windows – a medley of styles. A captivating feature on the right side of the structure is a deep three-story alcove, framed with corner boards capped in a charming design. The alcove serves to create a second and third floor balcony, a feature from the "Age of Romanticism."

Carol and Bruce Atkins are now the residents of this great house that lends prestige to Chestnut Street. They maintain the house as they bought it, divided by the Wescotts during the Depression into three spacious apartments.

Lynde House, 1881

130 Chestnut Street

"a fantasy delight for adults and children."
Michael Bloom, Architect

The remarkable feature of this late Victorian house is the elegant tower, one of the highest points in Haddonfield. On a clear winter's day, Philadelphia can easily be viewed from its windows. Reached by an interior winding stairway, it has been, according to its present owner, architect Michael Bloom, "a fantasy delight for adults and children alike."

The windows and louvers of the octagonal tower are capped with ornamented curved moldings and beautifully designed brackets rarely seen in Victorian towers.

The house was built by John D. Lynde on a lot bought by his wife, Cordelia on July 29, 1881 and was lived in by the Lyndes for 40 years until 1919. Mr. Lynde who owned a cast iron foundry incorporated many revolutionary technical ideas into the house in keeping with the Edisonian decade in which the house was built. He installed a low pressure steam central heating system; radiators were built into the walls with slits in the baseboard and the wall to provide air circulation. He also installed a large fan in the tower connected to a duct system which evacuated the hot air from the top of the high ceilings.

The house was built without a fireplace as testimony to the confidence Mr. Lynde had in his new heating system. The fireplace was added later in the rear parlor and connected to the old kitchen fireplace which was in the basement. The interior plan of the house is classic Victorian of the period, with two parlors and front and rear stairs. Ceilings on the first floor are 11 feet high, on the second, 10 feet, and on the third, 9 feet.

The original slate roof, the graceful porch posts and brackets with whimsical ornament, the dormers with characteristic Gothic windows have been preserved or restored to their original condition, including the removal of the aluminum siding which was put on in the 40's.

Among the notable features of this property is the original double hairpin fence with cast iron stars on each fence picket around the street perimeter. Each star proudly shows an L for Lynde's last name and was made at his foundry.

Thomas Redman House, 1834 (1755)

140 Westmont Avenue

Oh, Thomas was a valiant man,
Clerk of the Meeting he,
When he proclaimed the Meeting's sense
Not one would disagree
                    James Lane Pennypacker,
                    Ballad of 1777

Among the most illustrious early families of Haddonfield, the Thomas Redman family is a shining example of leadership in the religious, economic and social life of the budding village. The first Thomas Redman to settle in Haddonfield in 1730 was the son of Thomas Redman of Philadelphia, a leading mechanic in that city. Son Thomas had been apprenticed as a druggist and soon after settling in Haddonfield he opened the first drug store in the village on "King's Road," at what is now 211 King's Highway. Thomas died in 1766 and left several children, of whom Thomas Redman, 2nd, followed his father's business, and was also a conveyancer. He was a leader among the Friends and in the civic affairs of the community. In 1775 he became the proprietor of the Indian King Tavern, and sold the inn to Hugh Creighton on May 1, 1777, at the time the tavern was the scene of Revolutionary War events. It is reasonable to assume that he sold the inn as he refused actively to support the Revolution, for which he was jailed in Woodbury in 1777 for two months, where he kept a diary of his experience.

Thomas, 2nd bequeathed to his son, Thomas, 3rd, considerable means, which enabled him to acquire land for the Redman farm in West Haddonfield, which extended from the Ferry Road (Haddon Avenue) west to the Hinchman Farm (Hinchman Avenue) and from Euclid Avenue north to Crystal Lake Avenue. On the land was a small log house built about 1755 which Thomas Redman preserved and is now the rear portion of the 1834 mansion. The Thomas Redmans were noted for their hospitality in the new mansion, entertaining in style, and offered the Isaac Wood family its shelter when the Wood house at 201 Wood Lane was destroyed by fire in 1841, until their new home was built.

Besides the historical significance of the building, the interesting and unusual architecture for the period of the early 19th century commands attention. As befitting Quaker Thomas Redman, the house is plain, yet elegant, appropriate to a man of wealth, acquired through his own prosperous business and his marriage to Elizabeth Lord Hopkins, granddaughter of John Estaugh Hopkins, who lived at what is now 65 Haddon Avenue, and whose land holdings covered much of West Haddonfield.

The two and a half story stucco building has an early style gambrel roof, reminiscent of Haddonfield's and Redman's farming roots. The barrel vaulted dormers are set into the original standing seam tin roof. At the front in the crossing gambrel roof dormer is a small "pseudo" Palladian window with curving wood trim and fish-scale siding. The portico porch in colonial style appears to have been added later, but the later additions have been modestly done, including the six over one pane replacement windows, so that the original design of the building has not been destroyed. The house is a visible legacy of the distinguished Redman family.

Bell Farm House, 1885

591 Chews Landing Road

The shadows created by the porch are contrasted by the beauty and detail of the railings and hanging balustrade recently restored. Splendidly turned wood posts were discovered beneath square boxed covering, and recreated, guided by old photos.
Charles Weiler, AIA

This remarkable example of the Queen Anne style, built in 1885 on land originally part of the Bell Farm, is situated on one of the highest properties in Haddonfield. Not much imagination is needed to visualize horse and carriages traveling the dirt road of the late eighteen hundreds while sitting on the elegant wraparound porch, one of the most beautiful porches in the town. The house has all the charms of the Queen Anne style—the grand round corner turret, the angled bays, the hipped roof dormers and gables covered with decorative fish scale shingles. The round turret and conical slate roof add focus and emphasis to the building's main entry door, yet despite their massiveness, appear to be weightless over the grand scale of the porch.

Set back from the corner, the house sits quietly and calls to you from the past, in a bygone setting of huge mature trees. It is not difficult to see the house on the large farm owned by Ezra C. Bell, one of the most successful agriculturists of Camden County, a descendent of a long line of farmers, members of the Society of Friends, who settled in the last decade of the 17th century on lands purchased from William Penn. They settled in Montgomery County, Pa. and purchased 240 acres of land in 1847 in Union (now Centre) Township, Camden County. The land which came to Ezra Bell was the purchased tract of 71 acres and part of the original tract. Here he pursued the same intelligent system of agriculture, taking advantage of the use of machinery and the application of fertilizer. Bell built a house on the farm in 1856, believed to be made of clay tiles. He was still farming the land with seven acres under strawberries in 1883, but there is no record of whether he built the house that has survived today, which may have been built by one of his children, John H., Edwin R., Margaret C. and Caroline R. Bell.

Ezra Bell regarded education as applicable to farming as to mechanics, to merchandising as to the arts or sciences, a revolutionary concept in the nineteenth century. The Bell Farm house reflects a man of culture, an adherent of the virtue of Quaker simplicity in architecture as in other aspects of life. And so the Queen Anne vogue with all its exuberant charms is tempered by the Quaker influence which marks the character of most of the period houses in Quaker Haddonfield. The faithful restoration of the house is the achievement of Kay and Courtney Malcarney, present owners.

Above: *Stout-Field Houses, 1835,*
250 King's Highway East

Above: *Hendry-Pennypacker House, 1834,*
          255 King's Highway East

Above: *306 King's Highway East, 1860*

Above: *Evans House, 1890,*
 120 King's Highway West

Hopkins Pond

The sunlight streams through
* the tulips and oaks and beeches*
That shelter the pond,
And spatters with gold the quiet water-reaches,
And woodland and meadow beyond.

> Verse and Prose,
> James Lane Pennypacker, June, 1922

This picturesque historic landmark was formed from a small stream, a branch of Cooper's Creek. The dam was constructed in 1789 to provide water for the Haddon Mill which was built at the same time by John Estaugh Hopkins who had inherited 117 acres of woodland from his father, Ebenezer Hopkins, the beneficiary of Elizabeth Haddon's estate. The stone Mill was built by Major William Ellis, a Revolutionary War veteran, and his son-in-law Daniel Fortiner erected the dam. Five years later in 1794, John Estaugh Hopkins built the first home on the tract for his son William, who took over the management of the Mill. It was William's wife, Ann Morgan, who named the estate "Birdwood." The stone Mill is long since gone, but Hopkins Pond remains a treasured asset to the environs of Haddonfield.

Chronology of Historic Homes and Buildings

The following is a list of houses and buildings included in "Haddonfield Historic Homes," arranged according to date when built. In cases where a house or building has two dates, signifying the date of a later addition, as in the Aspden-Champion-Blackwood House, 1760-1846, the Reeves-Glover House, 1813-1835, and the Roberts-Mitchell House, 1865-1883, the earlier date is placed first if the earlier house became an integral part of the architecture of the later addition. The later date is placed first if the later addition was built on a portion of the

earlier building which is not in public view or part of the front facade, such as the Judge John Clement House, 1852-1743, and the Estaugh Inn, 1850-1740. This arrangement is to guide the viewer. For example, the dominant architecture of the Judge John Clement House, 264 King's Highway East, is the 1852 house he built on a portion of the original 1743 house, built by his granduncle Jacob Clement, which clearly marks the earlier colonial architecture and the later Gothic Revival architecture.

Early Architects and Builders

Architecture as a formal practice was not known until 1859, when the American Institute of Architects was formed. But architecture was not unknown to the master builders who designed their own buildings to meet the needs and desires of their clients. One didn't need an architect to design a building "historically." Clients and builders had access to builder's handbooks, books of designs by recognized architects, and enlightenment of European architecture learned in their native land or from journeys abroad. The architecture of a period is a direct reflection of that society's culture, and expression of the period in time. The master builders developed a following and sought to make their buildings more elegant. The magnificent architectural details of many of Haddonfield's houses are testimony to the integrity of their design and quality of their workmanship.

Haddonfield has been singularly fortunate to have had among its residents gifted, talented builders and skilled craftsmen—stone-masons, bricklayers, carpenters, painters and glaziers. Since the early homes were known for their owners, the names of many of these master craftsmen have been lost. But a few have been recognized. Following are examples of their work.

John G. Shivers
One of the earlier builders, his surviving buildings include the John Clement "Three Sisters" houses, 227-229-231 King's Highway East, beautiful examples of the Federal period style; Kay-Shivers houses, 434-436 King's Highway East.

Charles H. Shinn
Built the Alexander House, 1844, 264 King's Highway East, and other elegant houses of that period.

William Coffin Shinn
Son of Charles H. Shinn, moved to Haddonfield in 1862, commissioned a Captain of the Union Army of the United States that year when he was 24 years of age. A distinguished and well-loved resident of Haddonfield and the surrounding area, he was active in civic affairs, and became a member of the New Jersey Legislature from Camden County. Well educated, he worked with his father who owned and operated a lumberyard on Potter Street and with Colonel Jesse Peyton in the coal and lumber business. He owned several properties in Haddonfield, and built several of the town's most beautiful mansions. In 1873 he engaged nationally known architect, Samuel Sloan, to design three houses for his client, William Massey, a wealthy Philadelphian, founder and president of the Camden and Atlantic Railroad. These "Stick Style" houses were a radical departure from even the most elegant Haddonfield houses at the time, requiring exceptional skill to build their highly decorative detail.

William S. Capern
In the late 19th century, the builder/contractor who changed the appearance of many of Haddonfield's streets was this enterprising builder who bought large tracts of land in Haddonfield and claimed in his promotional brochures to have "constructed fully one-third of the structural operations that have taken place including most of the fine residences, the Baptist Church and the Masonic Hall..." He is responsible for many of the custom-designed houses on Washington Avenue, for the comfortable vernacular houses in the area of Chestnut Street, the large homes on Linden Avenue and West End Avenue. Capern houses stand today as monuments to his claim that "modern habitations are models of the advancement effected in architectural designing and the structural art; embracing all the latest up-do-date provisions for comfort, health and convenience." They were built to last, and they have, adding considerably to Haddonfield's rich and varied architectural heritage.

Historic Preservation in Haddonfield
"Struggle and Success"

Haddonfield is one of the most attractive communities I've ever seen. This is due primarily to the preservation and restoration of its historic structures. Haddonfield is a shining example that historic preservation is good business and works to improve all aspects of a community.

> Paul J. Taylor, Curator, Historic Sites
> Office of New Jersey Heritage, 1983

If you have read "This Pleasant Town," the early history of Haddonfield, in the opening pages of this book, you will be heartened by the following account of how this pleasant town was saved from the destruction of that which is the heart of its image-its historic character.

Three forces were named that made this a pleasant town—the character of the people who settled here, its advantageous location, and "above all, the strong determination of its citizens to maintain and preserve its basic values and tradition." This final chapter of *HADDONFIELD HISTORIC HOMES* provides the history of that citizen effort, a record which will not be lost, will not be misrepresented and will, we hope, be instructive to present and future generations of Haddonfield citizens, and to other towns struggling to save their historic heritage.

In an article by William Murtagh, first Keeper of the National Register of Historic Places, and the key speaker at the Preservation Society's 1986 celebration of the 15th anniversary of the establishment of the Historic District Ordinance, he wrote:

We have moved from a preoccupation with landmarks intellectually isolated from their environments to entities of local concern in our culture; we have moved from a preoccupation with museums to a concern for neighborhoods where people live; and we have moved from a patriotically zealous approach to history to a greater appreciation of aesthetics.

"PRESERVATION IS NEVER DONE"

That true statement was the headline in an editorial printed in the *New York Times* during Historic Preservation Week, May, 1980. The *Times* reminded us that:

Historic Preservation is more than saving old buildings. It is the mark of a country come of age. Until the arguments for quality, beauty and cultural heritage are understood as well as the economic and energy advantages of preservation, we will underestimate the full value received.

THE THREATS

In an 1899 map of Haddonfield, showing the houses and buildings that existed at that time, featured at the top of the map are drawings of eight of the grand 19th century mansions in the old part of the town. Five of these were demolished in the 20th century. Among these was the 28-room Victorian mansion on the six-acre estate of William D. Sherrerd and his wife Mary Eva Sherrerd,

Above: *In the 1870's, great mansions were already being converted to commercial use.*
"Braddock's" was located at the southeast corner of King's Highway East and Haddon Avenue.

built in 1873 by A.J.A. Sheets, and purchased by the Sherrerds in 1893. At the time it was demolished in 1964 it was the most opulent landmark of domestic architecture in the town. Destroyed were its magnificent tower, its turreted porches, a conservatory with a charming pool surrounded by blooming plants, an immense ballroom, its paneled walls lined with imported tapestries of jacquard needlepoint, the ceiling painted with cherubs, the Louis XVI rococo style everywhere.

Yielding to the wrecker's ball, the irreplaceable exterior and interior architecture of other great houses, which gave aesthetic elegance to the town, the charming porches with intricate lacy brackets, the cupolas and windowed belvederes, the beautiful woodwork and fireplace mantels—were replaced by gas stations, parking lots and buildings of no architectural merit. One by one, Haddonfield's landmarks and landscape were vanishing.

Equally destructive to the architectural heritage of this colonial town were the alterations to historic buildings. Beautiful porches with their delightful decorative details were removed, as were the cupolas, belvederes, roof observatories, fine brackets. Original wood siding in good condition was covered with synthetic materials—asbestos, aluminum and fake stone and brick siding. In the business district, 18th and 19th century residences were converted to commercial use with the resultant alteration of the front facade and interior, with no regard for preserving the original architectural excellence of the building. At the corner of King's Highway and Haddon Avenue were four gas stations, three full stations and a gas pump in front of "Braddock's" store which was converted from a magnificent Second Empire stone dwelling. On each of the other three corners the mansions were totally demolished.

Creeping commercialism was also diminishing the residential quality of the town. Residential Haddonfield with its lovely homes in the historic center of the town was being gobbled up for commercial retail and office use which necessitated exterior and interior alterations, and because of the local ordinance for off-street parking, the conversion of the "gardens, orchards and grass plots," an integral part of "this pleasant town," into rear yard, black-topped parking lots.

In 1960, Haddonfield faced another formidable threat—the introduction of the PATCO High-Speed Line. Though it met with the strongest opposition in the history of the town, expressed through the poll taken, through the public hearings when more than 500 residents turned out to voice their concerns of how the high speed transportation from Philadelphia to Lindenwold would change the character of the town, the PATCO line was built in 1969 with certain modifications demanded by the citizens, such as eliminating an overhead passage on historic King's Highway, but not yielding on the construction of a major parking lot for 1000 cars in the center of the town, which remains an eyesore to this day. The location of the station and parking lot at the entrance to the prime residential area of west King's Highway meant the demolition of more homes, and more disastrous, as the public feared, opened the door to developers who sought to capitalize on this convenient transportation to two metropolitan areas—Philadelphia and Camden—by planning high density, high rise buildings adjacent to the Hi-Speed Line. Of course, this meant the demolition of several of the most historically and architecturally significant buildings in the town—43-45 King's Highway West and 51-53 King's Highway West-properties included in this book. Self-interested local developers used the siren song that high rise apartments would increase tax ratables and therefore reduce residential taxes, and succeeded in placing the question of high rise apartments and office buildings on the ballot in a public referendum on November 3, 1969. The defeat of this referendum was due to the efforts of the Preservation Society which had been the "watchdog" of the community since its organization in 1966. Its methodology was to do careful research, obtain all the facts and get them to the public. This was accomplished in a flyer distributed to every household in Haddonfield. It quoted a Rutgers University study which showed that:

High tax-rate communities are almost without exception the more densely populated municipalities, and low tax-rate districts are generally characterized by low densities of population and property.

The flyer stated that a "yes" vote on the referendum:

will invite developers and profiteers to urbanize this beautiful, spacious, prestige residential town with overcrowding, more traffic congestion, parking lots, auto pollution and blight...will increase taxes for more schools and services.

The referendum was defeated overwhelmingly but developers did not give up. A Dallas, Texas conglomerate hired a local realtor to buy up every property on one square block adjacent to the High-Speed Line—from Linden Avenue to Estaugh Avenue, to Euclid Avenue. This

would include the two great Victorian mansions in this vulnerable location, the Benjamin Lippincott houses and the Samuel Wilkins houses. Fortunately, the Preservation Society learned of this plan and aborted it by appealing to the Planning Board to bring out for enactment the Historic District Ordinance they were studying as part of the Master Plan, which prohibits demolition of historic properties for six months, giving the board the opportunity to save the buildings. Ann Ward, chairman of the Planning Board at the time, recognizing the urgency of the matter, separated the Historic District proposal in the Master Plan so that it could be acted on months before the Master Plan was approved and a new general Zoning Ordinance written.

This was a decisive and triumphant victory for saving Haddonfield's historic homes. It was recognized in the media and Philadelphia Magazine included the successful effort in its April, 1972 issue devoted to "South Jersey." Recognition was given to Joan Aiken and the Haddonfield Preservation Society who...*did her homework and found a few loopholes to latch on to.* Haddonfield was described in the article as the *Princeton without a university.*

TAKING ACTION

By 1966 when the PATCO High-Speed line was assured, a few concerned citizens had the vision to see the "handwriting on the wall." They organized "The Society for the Preservation of Residential and Historic Haddonfield," and named as principals Dr. William J. Snape, a trustee of the Camden County Historical Society, Louis H. Goettelmann, architect and architectural historian, and David Miller, resident of Moore Lane, and charter members: Mrs. Edna Haydock, Mr. and Mrs. Louis H. Goettelmann, Mr. and Mrs. Henry D. M. Sherrerd, Mr. and Mrs. Sherrerd Massey, Mr. and Mrs. James Bontemps, Mr. and Mrs. Charles Sheppard, Mrs. Marjorie Richardson, Mrs. Caroline Moody, Dr. and Mrs. William J. Snape, Mr. and Mrs. James G. Aiken, Mr. and Mrs. David Miller. Joan Aiken, a public relations practitioner for many years, was named Chairman of Communications. The Society's goal was to develop ways and means of halting the further destruction of the residential and historic character of the town. The following year, in March, 1967, the Preservation Society took action to stop the proposed demolition of the handsome 19th century house at 134

King's Highway West, the MacNeil house, by a Catholic order, to build a larger convent for the nuns on the site. Three Society members, Louis Goettelmann, Joan Aiken and Edna Haydock appealed to the nuns to save the house and build an addition to meet their needs on the large grounds at the rear of the property, but the nuns were adamant. However, the Committee had an opportunity to see the splendor of the interior—the solid mahogany doors and woodwork, all the superb architectural details, which only strengthened their resolve to save the house.

In February, 1967, the Historical Society had been apprised by John Marter, the Borough Administrator, that the MacNeil house and the adjacent St. Mary's Academy building had been purchased by the Catholic Order of St. Mary of the Angels and it was decided that these houses were to be torn down at a later date or given to a person who could move them. The Society approved that a letter be sent to Mayor Franklin Fretz presenting its objections. But no action was taken until the demolition was imminent. On March 28, 1967, the Historical Society presented the Commissioners a petition of 57 names to use the zoning laws to save the buildings. This also proved a dead end. Mr. Goettelmann stated "This is a fine house and the more houses we tear down, the less it will look like a residential area." Commissioner George Farrell responded, "What can we do to keep houses from being torn down? Nothing." The petitioners were told "the Commission has no authority to stop the demolition. That right belongs to the owner."

It was the Preservation Society that reached for the last hope of saving the grand house–litigation. The Society's trustees and charter members filed suit against the borough and several officials, seeking an injunction to prevent demolition of the MacNeil house. The complainants in the suit were Henry D.M. Sherrerd who paid the costs of the litigation, Mr. and Mrs. Louis Goettelmann, Lois Sherrerd, William and Barbara Snape, James and Joan Aiken, Edna Haydock and Elizabeth Hopkins Lenhart, official historian for the Preservation Society. They were represented by James G. Aiken, Esquire, counsel for the Society. At a meeting it was decided to ask the Historical Society to join the complainants as it was thought that the support of a historical organization would have a positive effect on the outcome of the suit. At a Historical Society Board meeting, Louis Goettelmann, also president of the Historical Society, Joan Aiken, Bulletin Editor and Trustee, and

Elizabeth Lenhart, Trustee, were able to persuade the Board to join as one of the complainants.

The suit was filed April 13, 1967, but the legal effort failed. The decision in early May, handed down by Judge Orvyle Schalick, refused to grant a restraining order forbidding issuance of a demolition permit. The basis of his opinion was that there was no evidence of anything illegal having taken place to warrant issuance of a restraining order. The MacNeil house was razed that week. There was no public outcry. The only outcry came from the Preservation Society which moved hastily to take steps to develop and enact local historic preservation legislation. The Historical Society, though asked, refused to take on the project as it was a tax-free educational institution and it feared the controversial nature of historic preservation might jeopardize that status.

On May 12, 1967, just a few days after the demolition of the MacNeil house, The Preservation Society was incorporated as the "Society for the Preservation of Residential and Historic Haddonfield." The incorporators were William J. Snape, Barbara Snape, James G. Aiken, Joan Aiken, W. D. Sherrerd Massey, Elizabeth D. Massey, William E. Moody, Caroline B. Moody, Patricia Miller, David L. Miller, Lois Reeside Sherrerd, Henry D. M. Sherrerd, Marjorie Richardson, Edna L. Haydock and Louis H. Goettelmann.

The purpose for which the corporation was formed is stated in the corporation papers:

to promote generally and specifically the residential, historic, architectural and aesthetic appearance and character of the Borough of Haddonfield; to promote harmonious design and building, planting and landscaping of the said Borough, and specific property or properties within said Borough; and to eliminate or minimize offensive, noxious, hazardous and unaesthetic elements which affect or might affect the residential, historic, aesthetic and architectural character of the said Borough; and to pursue or bring any claim or claims, cause or causes of action relating to or affecting the general or specific residential, architectural, historic, or aesthetic character of said Borough or any property or properties therein situate and to urge or persuade any governmental unit, municipal, county, state or federal, on or about or in matters, action or actions, or legislation, relating to the general purposes for which this society is organized.

Several Committees were formed including those on

Zoning, Beautification, Programs and a Historic District Ordinance Committee, which took priority because of the disastrous experience with the MacNeil house and the anticipated problems stemming from the proposed High-Speed Line. Members of this Committee were Louis H. Goettelmann, chairman, architectural historian; Joan Aiken, research and communications; Elizabeth Lenhart, historian; and William Blake, photographer of historic houses, for a planned color slide presentation on "Preserving Historic Haddonfield."

After many months of research, study, and visiting other successful Historic Districts—Cape May (the only one at that time in New Jersey), Society Hill (Philadelphia), Savannah, Charleston, New Orleans, Joan Aiken drafted a 22-page recommendation to the Planning Board and the Commissioners. In this project, Joan Aiken was greatly assisted by Helen Bullock of the National Trust for Historic Preservation, by Margaret Tincom, chairman of the Historic Preservation Commission in Philadelphia, and the State Office of Historic Preservation (now the Office of New Jersey Heritage).

THE RECOMMENDATION STATED ITS PURPOSE:

...to develop and enact an ordinance for the purpose of preserving houses, structures, buildings and sites of historic or architectural significance.

...to establish a historic district in which such houses and structures exist in order to:

1. *create or preserve a harmonious environment for "Old Haddonfield."*

2. *safeguard the heritage of Haddonfield and that part of the town which reflects elements of its cultural, social and architectural history.*

3. *stabilize and improve property values*

4. *foster civic beauty*

5. *promote the use of a historic district for the education, pleasure and welfare of both the citizens of Haddonfield and its visitors.*

The recommendation set forth the threats to the historic character of the town, the need to protect this architectural heritage with historic preservation laws, and covered every aspect of historic preservation—economic, legal, cultural and aesthetic. The qualifications of every member of the Committee were given, and attached to the recommendation were three case histories (success stories) of other established historic districts-Savannah, GA., Charleston, SC, Cape May, NJ, with emphasis on the economic benefits to these towns.

The Preservation Society Committee requested time to make its presentation to the Planning Board, after the Board's regular meeting on January 20, 1970. The presentation included the showing of the color slides that had been taken of several dozen historic houses in the Borough and the proposed Historic District, with Louis Goettelmann describing the houses and their historic and architectural significance. The Committee asked that the Planning Board appoint the four members to develop a Historic District Ordinance for the Board's review. The enthusiastic reception of the Planning Board was extremely heartening to the Committee which had worked so hard for almost two years on this major research project. The Chairman of the Planning Board at that time was Robert Twitchell who appointed Richard Walter, member of the Board, to join the Preservation Committee in the development of the Ordinance.

INFLUENCING PUBLIC ATTITUDES

Meanwhile, the Preservation Society developed a "blueprint" for historic preservation success. Immediately after the demolition of the MacNeil House, the Society began a strong communications campaign to win the support of the public for historic preservation legislation for Haddonfield. It was a strange new field for all but a few staunch preservationists. Here is a brief outline:

May 10, 1967 — Letter to 500 residents recounting the disastrous outcome of the efforts to save the MacNeil house, and inviting them to attend a meeting on Wednesday, May 17, at Greenfield Hall, to hear the presentation of a constructive program to halt the further erosion of the historic character of their town. The Society introduced its purposes, named its trustees and charter members (all well-established people in the Borough) and asked for their support. The letter's appeal stated, "We all know that alone our voice means little, but joined with many other responsible citizens we can add authority to our demands that thoughtless destruction of our heritage be stopped."

June 7, 1967 — Letter to 500 residents requesting

membership in the new Society for Preservation of Residential and Historic Haddonfield, outlining the program for the 1967-1968 year. (1) To promote new legislation and enforce present laws to preserve Haddonfield's historic and architecturally notable homes and buildings; (2) to maintain and enhance residential property values throughout the Borough; (3) to encourage the highest standards of aesthetic beauty in all commercial and residential areas.

November, 1968 — Symposium on "Historic Preservation? - Pro and Con," held at the Haddon Fortnightly. The audience, by special printed invitation, included borough officials, planning and zoning board members, organization presidents, realtors, business and civic leaders, and was also open to the general public. Symposium speakers were Frederick Haupt, 3rd, director of public affairs for the National Trust for Historic Preservation, Jack E. Boucher, supervisor, Historic Sites, State of New Jersey and Louis H. Goettelmann, chairman of the Historic District Ordinance Committee of the Preservation Society. Mr. Haupt spoke on the "Profits of Preservation."

Mayor Franklin Fretz, who was completely negative about a Historic District Ordinance, was invited as guest of honor, in the hope that the speakers at the Symposium would change his mind. Each attendee received, as he entered the auditorium, a packet including a list of the number of historic houses which would be included in the Ordinance, the Criteria of Evaluation used by the National Trust for Historic Preservation and the National Register of Historic Places, and fact sheets in the form of questions and answers on the proposed Historic District for Haddonfield. A very large audience enjoyed the refreshments in the lovely tea room of the Fortnightly after the Symposium and had the opportunity to exchange views with others. Historic Preservation made many friends that evening. The phrasing of the subject of the Symposium was credited with the large turnout. "Pro and Con" offered the citizens of the town who were against historic preservation, as well as for it, a voice in the debate. It also offered the Preservation Society the opportunity to have authoritative speakers quell many of the fears and doubts that arose in this controversial issue.

March, 1970 - By 1970, the Preservation Society had 100 dues-paying members and was able to budget monies for a more ambitious communications campaign. The Society

therefore produced a four-page Supplement to the local weekly newspaper, the *Haddon Gazette*, which was distributed to most households in Haddonfield. The Supplement, "Preserving Historic Haddonfield," had an electrifying effect on the citizens of the town. The cover pictured two historic buildings and a map of the proposed Historic District. Pages two and three featured eighteen historic houses with thumbnail histories written by historian Elizabeth Lenhart. Included were a brief history of Haddonfield and the Criteria of Evaluation of the houses and buildings to be included in the Historic District. Most effective was the information on the back page—"Why Historic Preservation?" In boldface type, set off with its own headlines, were answers to the two most vexing objections expressed by various citizens:

"HOW HISTORIC PRESERVATION INCREASES TAX RATABLES," and

"ZONING CONTROLS BENEFIT ALL."

COMMUNICATIONS STRATEGY

By law, zoning ordinances must have a public hearing. The Planning Board is empowered to develop the zoning ordinance and zoning plan, but the elected officers, the Commissioners, have the authority to approve or deny. Therefore, the most critical hurdle to overcome was the public hearing on the Historic District Ordinance when the Planning Board was ready to present it to the public. The Preservation Society Historic District Ordinance Committee had delivered its draft of a Historic District Ordinance to the Planning Board as requested. The Planning Board was in the process of reviewing and refining the Ordinance. The Planning Board had been working on the borough's updated Master Plan for some time and had included "Setting aside a historic district," a point which, according to the *Courier-Post* news story, April 13, 1971, *...local interest groups have pushed for the past two years*. It was announced that June was the Master Plan release date.

A review of the introduction at a public hearing of Historic District Ordinances in many municipalities revealed that it was at this point that so many of them fail to adopt the local ordinance. Why? The public was not prepared. It is at the grass roots level, the opinion of the tax-paying citizens of the town, that historic

(continued on page 185)

PRESERVING HISTORIC
HADDONFIELD

MARCH 1970

Published by The Haddonfield Preservation Society — Box 192 — Haddonfield, N. J. — Member, National Trust for Historic Preservation

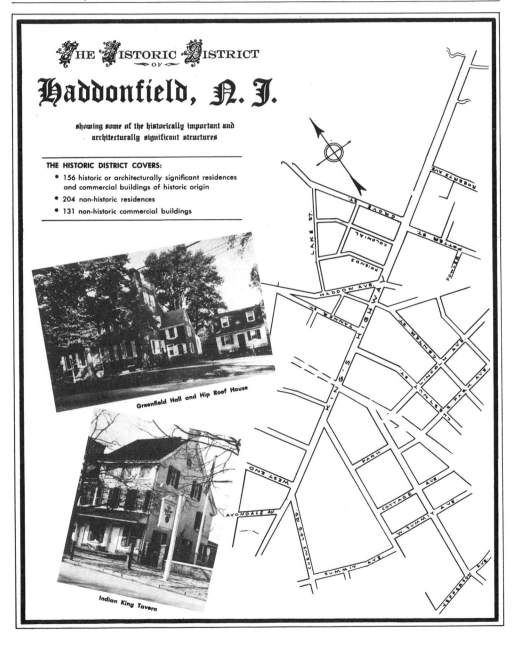

The Historic District
OF
Haddonfield, N. J.

showing some of the historically important and
architecturally significant structures

THE HISTORIC DISTRICT COVERS:
- 156 historic or architecturally significant residences and commercial buildings of historic origin
- 204 non-historic residences
- 131 non-historic commercial buildings

Greenfield Hall and Hip Roof House

Indian King Tavern

Above: *The importance of public education. This supplement to the HADDON GAZETTE appeared on Thursday, March 5th, 1970.*

Criteria Of Evaluation

The houses shown and described on these pages represent only a portion of the complete selection of historic and architecturally significant homes and buildings in Haddonfield.

The structures and sites on the entire list were selected by a noted architect and architectural historian, Louis H. Goettelmann, who is also president of the Haddonfield Historical Society and Chairman of the Historic Preservation Committee of the Haddonfield Preservation Society. Mr. Goettelmann's work on the Committee for the Restoration of Batsto, N.J., is well known.

We are more than fortunate that Mr. Goettelmann has given his services without fee to aid historic preservation for Haddonfield. The Criteria of Evaluation is that established by the National Trust for Historic Preservation, Washington, D.C.

Elizabeth Haddon
"Brew House"
201 Wood Lane
C. 1713

The original building erected by Elizabeth Haddon Estaugh, founder of Haddonfield. It escaped the fire which destroyed the mansion 30 feet away. It is not known precisely what year the Estaughs built this outbuilding which was used as a "laboratory" for Elizabeth Haddon's famed medical skills. Presumably it was built at the same time as the mansion or shortly thereafter. It is a beautiful example of early brickwork.

"Hip Roof House"

Fondly known as the "Hip Roof House," but misnamed as it actually has a gambrel roof, this small dwelling is said to have been built by Samuel Mickle, in the very early eighteenth century. It later became the property of Elizabeth Haddon, who willed it to her "kinswoman" Sarah Hopkins. Having been moved three times it has finally come to rest on the grounds of the Haddonfield Historical Society.

Our most important historical building, the Hip Roof House is registered in the Department of the Interior, Washington, D.C., having been selected by the Advisory Committee of the Historic American Buildings Survey as possessing exceptional historical and architectural interest and as being worthy of most careful preservation for the benefit of future generations. To this end a record of its present appearance and condition has been made and deposited for permanent reference in the Library of Congress.

CREDITS

HISTORY OF HADDONFIELD
"This is Haddonfield"
"The Life of Elizabeth Haddon" (Haddonfield Historical Society)
"The Two Hundredth Anniversary of the Settlement of Haddonfield" (Haddonfield Publication Committee)

PRESERVING HISTORIC HADDONFIELD
Haddonfield Preservation Society
National Trust for Historic Preservation

PHOTOS

William P. Stokes, Kingsway Photos

"PRESERVING HISTORIC HADDONFIELD" was prepared by the Historic Preservation Committee of the Haddonfield Preservation Society. Louis H. Goettelmann, Architectural Historian; Elizabeth H. Lenhart, Historian; Joan L. Aiken, Editor; William J. Blake, Photographs.

Shiver - French House
309 Kings Highway East
1758

This house was built on land formally owned by Elizabeth Haddon Estaugh, and was built by John Shivers. Originally two rooms wide and one room deep, and of brick construction the house contained two stories and a loft with an "A" roof.

Thackara House
24 Potter Street
C. 1819

Thought to be older, the earliest date we have on this house, from an old deed is 1819, when it was sold to one William Fortner. This deed shows the signatures of Thomas Redman Jr., Joseph Porter and Samuel Brown, commissioners.

Lake Street Meeting House
1760

Built on land given to the Friends by John and Elizabeth Estaugh on the site of an earlier log building previously used by the meeting.

"Birdwood"
Hopkins Lane
1794

Situated at the end of Hopkins lane overlooking the pond this lovely colonial home has been found by architects to be a duplicate in many respects to the house at Valley Forge which was used as Washington's headquarters during the Revolution. Built by John Estaugh Hopkins, great nephew of Elizabeth Haddon, for his son William Estaugh Hopkins, it remained in the family until recent years when it was purchased by former Governor of New Jersey, Alfred E. Driscoll.

34 Potter Street
C. 1810

Much research has yet to be done to ascertain the original deed, owner and date of construction of this early nineteenth century house which has been charmingly restored by the present owners.

Willits - Appleton House
22 Roberts Avenue

This beautiful picturesque house was built by Nathan Willits in 1836. It was moved from the Kings highway and restored in 1914 by Haddonfield architect Herbert R. Leicht, who resided there until his death in 1966.

Samuel Wood House
Wood Lane
1844

This house was built by Samuel Wood on the foundations of the original Elizabeth Haddon Mansion which was destroyed by fire in 1842.

The Story Of Haddonfield

Few early American towns have the romantic beginnings that have made the history of Haddonfield a never-ending delight to local historians and the inspiration of America's celebrated poet, Henry Wadsworth Longfellow.

Longfellow's beautiful tale of Elizabeth Haddon, who arrived in the new world in 1700 and founded Haddonfield in 1713*, evokes more than the hard, dry facts of history. We see this earnest, energetic, warm-hearted and devoutly religious girl with an exceptional intellect and lively imagination, a girl barely out of her teens, sent to America by her father to take up a parcel of his land and cast her lot with the unbroken wilderness.

Elizabeth was the eldest of three daughters of John and Elizabeth Haddon, well educated and genteel people, dedicated members of the Society of Friends, who resided in Southwark, England. John Haddon, who owned extensive lands in the new country reaching from Salem County to above the Falls of the Delaware, had an option on 500 acres of land on Cooper's Creek, bought from Thomas Willis on the condition that he take possession in six months. Unable to come here himself he sent his daughter Elizabeth with full power to transact business in his name.

Her mission was the fulfillment of her fondest dreams. Her imagination had been stirred by a visit in her childhood of William Penn to her father's house. Elizabeth was so engrossed with his tales of the Indians that for a time she played "Indian," named her doll Pocahontas, and designed a bit of leather to carry her kitten like a papoose.

These early pleasurable impressions no doubt account for her affection towards the Indians when she settled here and their reciprocation in a friendship charmingly epitomized in our Borough Seal.

When Elizabeth was eleven her parents took her to yearly Meeting where she heard among other preachers a young man, seventeen years of age, named John Estaugh of Kelvedon, Essex. Undoubtedly he made a strong impression on Elizabeth's heart and mind for shortly after she arrived in America and established her first home on the banks of Cooper Creek, a home to become the center of warm hospitality for visiting Friends, she met young John Estaugh again as a minister in the Society of Friends, and proposed marriage to him.

This proposal, recounted in Longfellow's poem, depicts the two young people on horseback on their way to Meeting in Salem. Elizabeth leans over in her saddle to fix a strap and is aided by John Estaugh. The rest of the company ride on. Then, according to Longfellow.

"Elizabeth said, though still with a certain reluctance,/As if impelled to reveal a secret she fain would have guarded,/ 'I will no longer conceal what is laid upon me to tell thee,/ I have received from the Lord a charge to love thee, John Estaugh.' "

They were married shortly thereafter and their marriage certificate, now owned by the Historical Society of Haddonfield, is the only document extant which bears the signature of Elizabeth Haddon

HADDON HALL OF HADDONFIELD

In 1713, twelve years after their marriage and some years spent in England, the Estaughs built a new brick house on a site now bounded by Merion avenue, Wood lane and Hawthorne avenue. It was called Haddon Hall of Haddonfield and marked the date of the founding of the village we now know by that

(Continued on Page 3)

John Estaugh Hopkins House
65 Haddon Avenue
1799

At the corner of Haddon avenue and Lake street, this house was built by John Estaugh Hopkins, great nephew of Elizabeth Haddon. in 1799. It is considered a beautiful example of colonial architecture. In the charming garden the original ice-house still stands.

David Roe House
32 Kings Highway West
1827

A magnificent white, late-Georgian house with exceptional architectural details. David Roe's daughter Florence married a noted village physician of the last century-- Dr. William Sumner Long. They and their son, the late William R. M. Long resided here, and it still remains in the hands of the family.

Greenfield Hall
343 Kings Highway East
1841

Now the home of the Historical Society of Haddonfield, this house was built by John Gill IV, in 1841, on the foundations of an earlier house built by John Gill II in 1749, one small wing of which remains and is used as the library of the Historical Society.

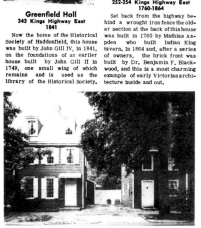

William Githens Houses
19 and 21 Potter Street
1829

Built on land purchased by Jacob Roberts from Isaac Kay in 1821 and sold to William Githens, cabinetmaker, in 1829, this quaint house and shop was faithfully restored by Mr. and Mrs. Lewis Barton.

Roberts Homestead
344 Kings Highway East
1816

Built on the former Kay property this handsome brick house was erected in 1816 by John K. Roberts, then owner of the Indian King tavern. Beautifully restored by its present owners this house proudly takes its place among the more distinguished homes on the Kings highway.

Hendry - Pennypacker House
255 Kings Highway East
1834

Built by Dr. Charles Hendry, son of the well known Dr. Bowman Hendry, and occupied by him for many years this gracious brick house was later purchased by Mr. James Lane Pennypacker, another well remembered and outstanding citizen of Haddonfield.

Aspden - Blackwood House
252-254 Kings Highway East
1760-1864

Set back from the highway behind a wrought iron fence the older section at the back of this house was built in 1760 by Mathias Aspden who built Indian King tavern. In 1864 and, after a series of owners, the brick front was built by Dr. Benjamin F. Blackwood, and this is a most charming example of early Victorian architecture inside and out.

Story

(Continued from Page 2)

name. The house stood until 1842 when it was accidentally burned to the ground. It was rebuilt in 1844 by Samuel Wood and now stands as an historic landmark at 201 Wood lane.

The only building now standing, originally constructed for Elizabeth Haddon is her Brew House, a "laboratory" for her famed medical skill, which stands about 30 feet from the rear of the Wood mansion. The fine old yew trees which she brought from England are still pointed out on the site where her extensive garden, celebrated for its herbs, vegetables and fruit once flourished.

The Estaughs were childless but had adopted Ebenezer Hopkins, the son of her sister Sarah. In her old age Elizabeth was surrounded by grandnieces and grandnephews.

John Estaugh died in 1742 at the age of 67 while on a religious visit to the West Indies. Elizabeth died on March 30, 1762, at the age of 82, and was buried in Friends Meeting graveyard on Haddon avenue. There is a tablet there in her memory, erected at the 200th anniversary of the founding of Haddonfield, in October, 1913.

Though Elizabeth became John Estaugh's wife the maiden name of Haddon survives in this community's history. In the last year's of Elizabeth's life, the village of Haddonfield had begun to be the centre of life for a growing population that sprung up around the great road (Kings highway) which had been early laid out from Burlington to Salem as a thoroughfare for wagon trains. Stores were opened, new occupations found a foothold. The community consciousness began to express itself in village institutions. Their needs gave rise to common endeavor and in this period, on March 8, 1764, the Haddonfield Fire Company was formed "consisting of a few men and two leather buckets apiece."

THE REVOLUTIONARY WAR
The peaceful quiet stream of life in this "greene countrie town" was rudely broken when the Colony of New Jersey joined with the others in their struggle for independence. During the Revolution Haddonfield was a place of some note. As a border town, it suffered indignities from both sides, one day in the hands of the Continentals, the next day the scarlet uniforms of the Kings troops. The Friends Meeting House was used as a hospital by each side in turn.

Though the inhabitants were mostly sound whigs, the town was loyal to the revolutionary cause. It raised its quota of troops and issued its own paper money to provide their equipment. Here Count Donop was quartered before the battle of Red Bank and with him a band of Hessians, outlandish in aspect and foreign in speech. They were succeeded by a Scotch regiment. Colonel Ellis stayed for a time and Anthony Wayne, Count Pulaski and Lafayette were familiar figures in its streets. And along Kings highway -- as though in the irony of history -- marched the British Army in its evacuation of Philadelphia.

THE INDIAN KING
"Whatever the village is the centre of, the inn is the centre of the village." Elizabeth Estaugh early opened a tavern house for the accommodation of travellers. This was followed by several others but the best known is the one bearing the name of the "In-

(Continued on Page 4)

*The date of the founding of Haddonfield, 1713, is derived from the year Elizabeth Haddon Estaugh built her brick house on the land now known as Wood lane. Her first home, when she arrived in America in 1700, was on the banks of Cooper Creek in the area presumed to be what is now known as Coles Mills, which became part of Haddonfield only in recent times.

Nathan Willits House
8 Kings Highway West
1836

Built by Nathan Willits. A distinguished 19th century house with an unusually beautiful Boxwood garden.

38 Haddon Avenue
1856

Built on land originally owned by John Estaugh Hopkins, and said to have been built around or on the site of an early log building which was once the Friends meeting which has been moved across the street. The right wing, added in 1933, is an authentic reproduction of an 18th century room with many original details.

132 Warwick Road
C. 1865

A very fine example of early Victorian architecture in Haddonfield, beautifully restored. It is now the Presbyterian Home.

The Evans House
120 Kings Highway West
1890

An elegant example of late Victorian architecture with French influence in the Mansard roof. Built by Ellwood Evans, father of Charles H. Evans, both former Commissioners of Haddonfield. Mr. and Mrs. Charles H. Evans reside there.

Why Historic Preservation?

As you enter the Borough of Haddonfield, you are greeted by a sign which reads, "Welcome to Historic Haddonfield founded 1713."

The sign, attractively designed in colonial style and bearing a silhouette of the Borough Seal symbolizing its founder, Elizabeth Haddon, was erected in 1963 by the Borough Commission under the direction of Mayor Albert B. Sharp to commemorate the 250th anniversary of the founding of Haddonfield.

The sign is also a symbol of the great pride officials and residents have felt throughout its 257 years in preserving and perpetuating the historic character of this venerable town, one of the few surviving authentic, "living" colonial towns in the nation.

The visible evidence of the history of a community is in its architecture. Without the preservation of its historic and architecturally significant homes, buildings and sites, there would be nothing left to see of that history except, as one resident put it, "The pictures on the Borough wall." The sign "Welcome to Historic Haddonfield" would then become a hollow legend.

It is this visible history and culture which gives Haddonfield its uniqueness and distinction, whose delightful physical characteristics create an authentic, harmonious and classic architectural environment we all know and enjoy.

There are also very practical advantages to preserving the old part of Haddonfield with its rich historic traditions. It undoubtedly attracts people of taste and cultural interests, people who come here to build, buy or restore homes of a caliber that have made Haddonfield one of the most desirable residential communities in the entire state. Our property values have remained among the highest. Our real estate and business fraternity have capitalized on "Historic Haddonfield" as a selling tool.

Now Haddonfield stands to lose this charming traditional character. Proximity to Camden and Philadelphia with their burgeoning populations seeking to escape urban ills, high speed transportation which brings urban sprawl ever closer -- all increase the pressures of developers and promoters to profit by the desirable location and atmosphere of Haddonfield, and consequently pose a threat to the historic, and still village-like, beauty of the town.

Unless we enact historic preservation laws there is nothing to prevent the demolition of all or part of this irreplaceable heritage. Much of it has already been lost to parking lots, gas stations, and inharmonious replacements. And only historic preservation laws can stop the tasteless, demaging and mutilating alterations of some of our architectural treasures, tragically apparent to all of us.

Haddonfield is not alone in seeking this solution to the problem. There are now 58 historic towns across the nation which have by municipal ordinance established an Historic District and an Historic District Commission to execute the ordinance.

Both the Federal and State governments have passed legislation to enable municipalities to take steps to halt this further loss of our historic landmarks and architecturally significant structures. President Nixon has given his unqualified endorsement and support to this legislation as an important contribution to the quality of our environment.

HADDONFIELD HISTORIC DISTRICT ORDINANCE

Accordingly, the Haddonfield Preservation Society undertook a two-year study for the purpose of establishing an historic district for Haddonfield. Its proposal was made to the Borough Planning Board on April, 1969. That Board appointed a sub-committee comprised of members of the Society to work with Mr. Richard A. Walter, vice-chairman of the Board to develop an Historic Preservation Ordinance. That ordinance is now before the Board.

Its purposes are:

1. to safeguard the heritage of the Borough of Haddonfield by preserving that part of the Borough which reflects elements of its cultural, social, economic and architectural history: (2) to maintain and develop an appropriate and harmonious setting for the historic and architecturally significant buildings, structures and places within that part of Haddonfield; (3) to stabilize and improve property values; (4) to foster civic beauty; (5) to promote the use of the historic district for the education, pleasure and welfare of the citizens of the Borough and its visitors.

Questions And Answers On The Proposed Historic Haddonfield

QUESTION: What will an Historic District do for Haddonfield and for the owners of property therein?

ANSWERS: 1. It will make possible the preservation of that part of Haddonfield which is characterized by attractive old houses and other historic buildings and sites from the eighteenth and ninetheenth centuries, and notable architectural examples of the twentieth century which contribute to the beauty and architectural harmony of the Historic District (such as the Fire House at 15 Haddon avenue which was built in 1952 on the site of the original fire house erected in 1764).

2. It will make Haddonfield an even more attractive place in which to live because residents will be secure in knowing

a. that the village quality will be protected as the general area becomes more urbanized;

b. that new housing and new businesses constructed within the Historic District will conform in architectural design to the special character of Haddonfield.

c. that the houses and property of their neighbors will continue to be attractive and that such alterations, improvements, restorations which are made by their neighbors will be in the spirit of the asthetics of the district and its historic atmosphere;

d. that the spirit of community pride will be fostered by the existence of the Historic District and that such pride will result in civic gains to their mutual benefit;

e. that an important step toward control will have been taken by the adoption of an Historic District;

f. that they, the present generation of residents, have held faith with the historic heritage of Haddonfield and have done right by their children and their children's children by being responsible trustees of the land and houses that are presently in their keeping.

3. It will enhance property values. Experience in other historic districts has demonstrated that the resale value of houses therein has risen as much as 30 percent to 300 percent.

QUESTION: How will the Historic Commission control the appearance of the district?

ANSWER: The Commission will pass on all future exterior changes to be made on buildings in the District working from an historical and architectural point of view. According to the Historic Commission Act, establishment of an historic district requires control only over the "exterior architectural features." This Act, now in effect in a growing number of other cities, towns and municipalities, permits owners to do what whey wish with the interiors and with the backs of buildings, and with any hidden outbuildings or any land to the rear. Even in areas which do show from the road, general repairs, maintenance, upkeep and landscaping which do not alter the basic architectural design are unrestricted.

QUESTION: Must all new structures and new additions be "colonial" in design?

ANSWER: Not necessarily. Any proposal must be aesthetically in keeping with the character of the District. As long as new construction is harmonious with that character and does not do violence to the architectural mood of nearby structures, the Commission will tend to support new designs.

QUESTION: Are houses of recent construction included in the District?

ANSWER: Inevitably newer buildings will fall within the boundaries of the Historic District. They will be subject to the same controls and the same protection and advantages as the older buildings.

QUESTION: What architectural help could a property owner expect from the Commission?

ANSWER: Without any attempt to bind the Commission to be appointed after the District is established, it is the experience of other such Historic District Commissions that those appointed are qualified and are glad to give detailed advice about design to householders and/or contractors who plan restorations, renovations, additions or new structures.

QUESTION: Will it be hard to sell houses inside the District? Suppose a prospective buyer does not want to be bound by the restrictions of the Historic District?

ANSWER: Experience all the way from Sante Fe, New Mexico to Beacon Hill, Boston has demonstrated that there is a positive demand for houses in historic districts. Prospective buyers tend to want the protection which an historic district will provide. It gives them the security of knowing that the neighborhood is quaranteed agains future deteriorations, urban blight or unattractive businesses. The fact that a house inside an historical district may sell for considerable more than a comparable house outside is evidence enough of this buyer demand.

QUESTION: What about business opportunities in an historic district?

ANSWER: Established businesses are certain to prosper. We have demonstrated in Haddonfield that increased prestige and attractiveness to shoppers has gone to business district since the voluntary "colonialization" of that district, long a model for other towns. New businesses which conform in architectural style which offer appropriate services to a residential community may well enjoy similar success. The Borough of Haddonfield's Zoning Ordinance, of course, controls where business may and may not be established. The Historic District control is limited to architectural appropriateness.

With the establishment of an Historic District there will be firmer controls over the business district which is a part of the Historic District area and thus minimize the likelihood that new businesses will not accept the voluntary colonial conformity or that urban pressures will demolish historic sites or structures in the business district.

The inclusion of the business area in the proposed Historic District will further promote and preserve Haddonfield's favorable colonial image. It will be a protection for the established businesses who have spent considerable money and effort to create an architectural harmony and attractiveness. Businessmen can capitalize on shopping in Haddonfield's Historic District, a unique attraction not shared by modern shopping malls.

ZONING CONTROLS BENEFIT ALL

A frequently heard objection to Historic Preservation zoning is that it restricts owners from "doing what they please" with their property.

If you stop and think about this, you will realize that all zoning is restrictive, all zoning tells us what we can or cannot do with our property.

We have a restrictive fence ordinance, sign ordinance, parking lot ordinance, height ordinance, sub-division ordinance, etc., etc. All are designed to enhance the physical appearance of the town. We have stringent use ordinances for the same reason.

Anyone who wishes to live in a community free from zoning restrictions should take a look at the uglification of our towns, cities and highways before such controls.

Zoning for aesthetics and zoning for historic preservation are now urged by all professional planning experts. Experience shows that many of those who demand "freedom from controls" are motivated by a desire to make a "fast buck" at the expense of the quality of the community environment, which is the total public good.

HOW HISTORIC PRESERVATION INCREASES TAX RATABLES

Residents and owners of property in historic districts are assured against deterioration of the area. Experience has demonstrated there is a positive demand for houses and commercial dwellipgs in historic districts. Surveys made show that property values increase anywhere from 30 to 300 per cent.

A typical example is Annapolis, Md., which just completed an independent study of the Annapolis Historic District, soon to be published, which points out that since 1961 the growth on true value of properties in the historic area has risen from an estimated level of $18,000,000 in 1961 to the current figure of $38,000,000 — an increase of 112 per cent. Tax assessments have risen 85 per cent. Historic Preservation can well be the solution to Haddonfield's decreasing business activity.

John A. Swinkler Home 34 Warwick Road 1825

Story

(Continued from Page 3)

dian King." It was built by Mathias Aspden. Within its walls the Colonial legislature gathered thrice and at the last session substituted the word "state" for the word "colony" in the documents of the new commonwealth. The Committee of Public Safety also met here.

A center of social life, its hospitable tables groaned under feasts of game, the taproom was filled and the music of the fiddle coupled with young feet dancing and joyous laughter reverberated from the ballroom above. Amid the numerous guests who frequented the lively dances none lingers with such fame and admiration as the winsome Dolly Madison.

The Indian King is now preserved as an historic landmark by the State of New Jersey.

THE CALL OF HISTORY

In all the many accounts of the history of Haddonfield, none expresses so sentiently the trust handed down to us who live here today by those who built and conserved this exceptional American community, as those of Frank Austin Smith, who delivered the historical address at the 200th anniversary of the founding of Haddonfield in 1913: "Here in this place of simple trust, in these fields of gentle living and noble desires, let us kindle the undying hope that those who come after us will keep from decay and ruin these places of historic memories.

(continued from page 180)

preservation zoning can succeed or fail. The Preservation Society therefore expended all its efforts in reaching the citizens of the borough with authoritative information on the benefits of historic preservation to the individual citizen, whether he or she lived in the proposed District or outside of it.

In the Society's contact with its helpful source of information, Helen Bullock of the National Trust, it became clear that the most effective approach to the public was on the basis of economics—dollars and cents. As a result, prominent speakers were invited to a series of programs sponsored by the Society giving indisputable evidence of the economic benefits of preserving the historic character of the town. The names and offices of these authoritative speakers and the subject of their talk are listed in the outline that follows, "Mobilizing Public Opinion for Historic Preservation." The prominence of the speakers and the public interest content of their talks made news and all the local and regional newspapers reported the event.

During the year 1970-71, a series of feature articles appeared in the local weekly newspaper, *Haddon Gazette*, recounting the story of other historic towns and their experience and success in historic preservation. The articles were written by Joan Aiken after her visits to these towns and interviews with their historic preservation leaders. Among these were New Orleans, the oldest Historic District in the country, Charleston, Savannah, Nantucket Island, and Cape May, the first municipality in New Jersey to enact a Historic District Ordinance. Haddonfield was the second.

In the early years of historic preservation, there was a great struggle to win public acceptance. It was a controversial, almost revolutionary idea, to mandate regulations, set standards, for private properties in order to save them from demolition or alteration. Important historic towns like Newport, Rhode Island, and even New Jersey's Cape May, had especially bitter experiences in winning that struggle and could not have done so without the heroic efforts and leadership of Annette Downing in Newport and Carolyn Pitts in Cape May. Therefore, Preservation organizations had, at first, little clout in historic communities.

The Haddonfield Preservation Society included in its communications strategy to win public support, the endorsement of well established and respected civic organizations. This was easier said than done because these organizations had to be convinced of the merit of Historic Preservation and had to have the courage to endorse a highly controversial issue. The shining example of support came from the Haddon Fortnightly, during the presidency of Ruth Wiggins, and the chairmanship of Aileen Blosser of the Community Improvement Committee of the Fortnightly. In 1970 the Committee at the request of the Society chose as its program "to work to rejuvenate the King's Highway business districts, and to support the campaign to establish a historic district in Haddonfield."

Mrs. Blosser's Committee also set up a meeting with members of the business community on May 26, 1971, to discuss "The creation of a Historic District in Haddonfield: what it will do for the business community and how it works." The Preservation Society, as part of the program, gave its color slide presentation, "Preserving Haddonfield's Historic Homes." The response was gratifying. From an attitude of total negative, many in the business community became supportive.

Every effort was made to win the endorsement of the Historical Society. Despite approval of the Historic District Ordinance by some of its members and most ardently by its president, Louis H. Goettelmann, and several of the members of Board of Trustees, there was no clear mandate of approval from the Historical Society as a whole. In the November, 1968 Bulletin of the Society, editor Joan Aiken reported excerpts of the talk by Frederick Haupt, director of public affairs for the National Trust for Historic Preservation, on the subject "Profits of Preservation," presented at a symposium on November 6, sponsored by the Haddonfield Preservation Society. Here was powerful persuasion by an authority on the benefits of historic preservation. At the July, 1969 meeting of the Historical Society, it was voted to poll the membership on the enactment of the Historic District Ordinance. President Louis H. Goettelmann told the members that "The support of the Haddonfield Historical Society in this vital and urgent program would be a major factor in the decision by our official body to make this preservation a law. Wherever it is a law, it has stabilized and increased property values in the historic district, a benefit to all those living in the district and the treasury of the borough." The poll was taken and a majority of members voted in favor of the endorsement.

Meanwhile, "Letters to the Editor" appeared for and against the Historic District Ordinance. In every case the "against" letters based their opposition on misinformation or misapprehension. These gave the citizens who were

The Public Hearing

When in April, 1971, the entire square block of properties west of the High-Speed Line was destined for demolition by the Dallas, Texas conglomerate who had hired a local realtor to buy up all properties, to be replaced with high rise apartments, the Preservation Society pleaded with the chairman of the Planning Board, Ann Ward, to hold a public hearing on the Historic District Ordinance alone, rather than wait until the total Master Plan hearing which included a proposal for a historic district. Recognizing the urgency of the matter and the determination to save a prime historic-residential area of the borough, Ann Ward and other members of the Planning Board voted to hold a public hearing on June 7, at Borough Hall. Afterward they planned to take a formal vote on the resolution. If the planners at that time approved the Historic District resolution it would be forwarded to the Commission for action. It is to the great credit of Ann Ward, Robert Twitchell and Richard Walter who made the excellent presentation of the Historic District Ordinance at the public hearing. And it is to the credit of the Haddonfield Preservation Society which had spent almost four years in educating the public on the benefits of historic preservation and the Historic District Ordinance. Because of these factors, there was very little opposition to the Ordinance and any questions from the audience were expertly answered by the Planning Board members.

As a result, the Planning Board approved the resolution and forwarded its decision to the Commissioners with the request to act on the Ordinance in sixty days, which would be the fourth Tuesday in August, at the regular meeting of the Commission. But the preservationists were prematurely jubilant. Despite the approval of the Planning Board and the support of the public, the Commissioners failed to approve the Historic District Ordinance at their August meeting. Prepared for any eventuality, the Preservation Society representative, Christopher Glennon, announced at that meeting that the question would be placed on a public referendum on the November 2 election ballot. This meant that more than 700 signatures had to be obtained to qualify for placing the question on the ballot. There was also a deadline for obtaining the signatures. Preservation Society members took on the burdensome job of knocking on doors, requesting signatures from shoppers on the sidewalks of King's Highway, explaining the question and the Ordinance to all. More than the required number of signatures were obtained and the question was placed on the ballot. The question was fashioned by the Preservation Society: "Shall the ordinance proposed by petition and prepared and recommended by the Haddonfield Planning Board to the Commissioners entitled 'An Act creating an Historic District in the Borough of Haddonfield' be adopted?" The inclusion of the recommendation of the Planning Board was very important as this gave official authority to the question.

The Opposition

The basis of the Commissioners' opposition to the Historic District Ordinance was that it was not legal. The Solicitor of the Borough advising the Commissioners was Albert Sharp who ignored all evidence to the contrary— evidence which the Preservation Society had carefully researched and presented to the Commissioners, and which the Planning Board had independently researched. The Land Use Law clearly included "Historic Sites" in granting authority for zoning to the Planning Board. Mr. Sharp interpreted this to mean a single historic site like the Indian King Tavern or the Princeton Battlefield. This was not the interpretation of the Office of Historic Preservation, New Jersey Department of Environmental Protection. "Historic Sites" could be a historic district.

The real estate fraternity opposed the Ordinance because it feared if restrictions were placed on properties the market value would be diminished or those properties wouldn't sell at all. One of the leading realtors in the town threatened that if the Commissioners enacted the Ordinance, he would sue the Borough.

Mayor Eugene Hinski had a very different view of the future of Haddonfield. At the time the Historic District Ordinance was being debated, the competition of neighboring shopping malls had dealt a severe blow to Haddonfield's business community. A number of the stores were empty and the Commissioners had permitted several to be converted to office use. Mayor Hinski, in a speech to the Rotary Club in Camden, declared:

(continued on page 192)

for the ordinance an excellent opportunity to reply with the correct information and interpretation of the ordinance.

TO THE CITIZENS OF HADDONFIELD

Why you should vote **NO** on the proposed Historic District

1. Discrimination

Taking away individual property owner rights of a minority group of citizens.

2. Unfair & Restrictive

Requires one person to conform to dictates of a few but allowing his neighbor to do as he pleases.

3. Illegal

After exhaustive study by commissioners and boro solicitor it was determined that there is no enabling legislation in N. J. for such an ordinance.

4. Jeopardizes

Present zoning ordinance. There is legal opinion to support the possibility that a successful lawsuit against the proposed historic district ordinance may very well cause the entire zoning ordinance to be declared invalid.

5. Taxes

Must increase thruout entire town because of an increase in ratables, thereby working hardships on many local residents, especially senior citizens and young families.

A VOTE **NO** WILL SUPPORT THE DECISION OF OUR BOROUGH COMMISSIONERS AND BOROUGH SOLICITOR AGAINST THIS **DISCRIMATORY** ACT.

Paid for by a concerned group of property owners, Haddonfield, N. J.

Above: *On Thursday, October 28th, five days before the November 2nd referendum, the above advertisement appeared in the* Haddon Gazette.

PRESERVING HISTORIC
HADDONFIELD

October, 1971

Published by The Haddonfield Preservation Society — Box 192 — Haddonfield, N. J. — Member, National Trust for Historic Preservation

THIS ... or MORE OF THIS ...

IN THE BEAUTIFUL HISTORIC AREA OF HADDONFIELD?

THE FRANCES CAREY HOME at 38 Haddon avenue, built in 1856 and restored by its owner, a renowned expert in American design, is jeopardized by the adjacency of a huge, incompatible, urban-type office building and a parking lot for 90 cars. Zoned for office use, its survival as a beautiful residence with office (as Mrs. Carey used it for her antique business) is precarious. Who wants to live next to a parking lot and overpowering commercial building? Yet our historic residential properties in our central area enrich the whole atmosphere of the town, and especially our business community. Only the Historic District Ordinance can save this house from eventual destruction and alteration of its magnificent architectural details.

REAR OF THE HUGE NEW OFFICE BUILDING on Haddon avenue in view of the historic Carey home and adjacent to the Library and other historic structures. Asphalt and parking for 90 cars replaced the open green space that might have been a mini-park and extension to the Library. The water table in this area may be seriously affected as heavy rains have no land to run off. Although the offices in this building are only half occupied, the parking lot is almost filled. Where will the additional cars park at full occupancy? The historic homes in the area cannot survive with these high density buildings, parking lots, more traffic congestion, noise. They will have to sell for more and more big office buildings.

A VOTE FOR THE HISTORIC DISTRICT ORDINANCE IS A VOTE FOR PROTECTION OF YOUR PROPERTY INVESTMENT IN A BEAUTIFUL HISTORIC-RESIDENTIAL TOWN . . . FOR PRESERVATION OF OUR HISTORIC ARCHITECTURAL HERITAGE, OUR GREATEST COMMERCIAL AND RESIDENTIAL ASSET . . . FOR CONTROL OF MORE BIG OFFICE BUILDINGS,

OTHER HIGH DENSITY USES IN OUR HISTORIC CENTRAL AREA . . . FOR CONTROL OF TRAFFIC CONGESTION, POLLUTION . . . FOR REJUVENATION OF OUR BUSINESS DISTRICT . . . FOR INCREASE IN TAX RATABLES THAT WILL ENHANCE THE QUALITY OF LIFE IN HADDONFIELD, NOT INVITE URBAN SPRAWL AND SUBURBAN BLIGHT.

VOTE YES
NOVEMBER 2

on the local ballot question:

"Shall the ordinance proposed by petition and prepared and recommended by the Haddonfield Planning Board to the Commissioners entitled "An Act Creating an Historic District in the Borough of Haddonfield" be adopted?

Above: *The 4-page supplement by the Haddonfield Preservation Society which appeared in the* Haddon Gazette *on Thursday, October 28th, five days before the November referendum.*

ANNAPOLIS MAYOR CREDITS HISTORIC PRESERVATION WITH 112 PERCENT INCREASE IN PROPERTY VALUES... "GOOD FOR BUSINESS AND GOOD FOR THE COMMUNITY AS A WHOLE."

WHAT OTHER MUNICIPAL OFFICIALS SAY ABOUT HISTORIC PRESERVATION

(Before Annapolis, Md., passed its Historic District Ordinance in a public referendum, the town had many of the same problems as Haddonfield -- a failing business district threatened by strong competition from surrounding shopping malls.)

(From PRESERVATION NEWS, April, 1971)

"Annapolis, Md., is one of the few cities where downtown property values have risen in recent years. This increase -- $8 to $10 million a year -- is largely credited by Annapolis Mayor Roger W. Moyer to the success of preservation efforts there.

"ANNAPOLIS IS DOING SOMETHING RIGHT," responded the Annapolis Evening Capital in a February 28 editorial. "Preservationists constantly and effectively contended that their aims were consistent with the goal of revitalizing commercial activity in the city. The logic of the argument is quite simple: attractive downtown residential neighborhoods encourage and inspire businessmen to maintain their property in a manner befitting the local environment...

"Annapolis has discovered that in terms of (municipal) improvement, it is absolutely essential that citizens, public officials and merchants work in harmony in order to build and maintain a compatible and enriching atmosphere.

"WE DO KNOW THAT THIS CITY IS DOING SOMETHING RIGHT BY TAKING THE APPROACH THAT PRESERVATION IS GOOD FOR BUSINESS, AND GOOD FOR THE COMMUNITY AS A WHOLE."

WHAT HADDONFIELD RESIDENTS SAY ABOUT HISTORIC PRESERVATION.

"All over the country citizens are trying to save our forests, our rivers, and are restoring homes and towns. It is not only legal but necessary if we wish to pass on to the next generation a world in which they can survive and of which they can be proud.

"Let us care and think about the majority of people in Haddonfield who partake the current effort for reparation its strong assent to the historic district.

"I grew up near Annapolis, Md., and watched it deteriorate. If any of you could have witnessed how much that town has improved since it has had an historic district, you would believe in this as much as I do."

Mrs. Robert J. Moore
614 Redman avenue

"The general public attitude about the (historic district) legislation seems to be torn between people who have the foresight to preserve an architectural heritage and those who desire short term gain from commercial construction. At the rate of current progress, we had better photograph what's left of the past and put it on file for reference by posterity at the town library.

"Failure for the historic zone legislation to win on election day will have long range, catastrophic effects on not only the people living here today, but those in the future as well. All those who do not vote or who vote against it will have contributed to the growth of building schemes that, at best, have a life expectancy of 25 years. Our society is becoming conditioned to a building cycle in which the owners pay for, make profit, tear down and build something new in a span of a very few years.

"I, for one, cannot believe that the majority of people in Haddonfield will permit the current drive for reparation its strong assent to the historic district.

"In years to come to replace our architectural heritage is our biggest asset from both a residential and commercial point of view. Chestnut Hill, just across the Delaware River, is a prime example of the rejuvenation that can happen to a commercial district with the right kind of planning and civic leadership.

"Don't contribute to the goals of a few opportunists. They're here today and gone tomorrow...just like the offices they build."

Ronald E. Shaffer
8 Roberts avenue
(owner of the historic Daniel Fortiner House, 1820)

THE HISTORIC DISTRICT ORDINANCE IS PROTECTIVE, NOT "RESTRICTIVE"

All zoning for civic beauty and a quality environment is protective of our property investment in creating a more desirable town in which to live. The entire spirit of our present Zoning Ordinance is towards aesthetic zoning. We have "restrictions" as to size of lot, building area and height to create a more spacious, uniform appearance throughout our town. We have "restrictions" for size, placement and lighting of signs in our commercial and residential districts. Towns which do not are an eyesore! We have a fence ordinance restricting height of fences to insure a more orderly, open appearance. New parking lots must be screened with a fence or shrubbery.

The proposed Historic District Ordinance sets design standards and guidelines for exteriors in front public view only. These guidelines will greatly enhance the property values of both historic and non-historic structures in the District. If there is any doubt see the restored historic homes: 22 and 8 Roberts avenue; 19, 21, 34 Potter street; 432, 434, 436 Kings highway east. Their market value is many times more than comparable houses in the area that have not had the benefit of these architectural standards. Remember, authenticity need not cost any more. It does insure the best appearance for your money.

It is these architectural standards, and the unity and harmony they create in an historic area, which delights us in such famous Historic Districts as New Orleans, Charleston, Savannah, Georgetown, Nantucket, Newport, San Antonio, and Society Hill, and many others.

Do we, in Haddonfield, not have the same pride to preserve our history and beauty?

WHAT EXPERT PLANNERS SAY ABOUT HISTORIC PRESERVATION

(From Graham W. Finney, Deputy Director Philadelphia City Planning Commission)

"Public controls such as height limit, design controls, and historic zoning districts are looked upon as impediments (by developers) to producing highest economic use. But in fact many controls are incentives to higher uses nearby. Until the Society Hill development began in Philadelphia, no development interest existed along the entire waterfront. Today this area has spurred major new construction and fantastic real estate values. Properties which sold for $2,000 in 1950 now sell for $100,000. Many Americans anxious to purchase "that colonial house" in Levittown can now purchase for the first time a REAL colonial house in Society Hill.

"The land adjacent to the historic areas has sky-rocketed in value. The 'rigid restriction' in preserving history has encouraged rather than discouraged more profitable development. Historic preservation can encourage proper location of this development."

A Local Businessman Says ...

Open Letter to the Haddonfield Planning Board:

As you may know, we recently purchased and refurbished the building at 232 Kings highway, (Samuel Reeves House) which dates from the year 1813.

As businessman we feel that the preservation of the historic character of Haddonfield has proven and will continue to prove of great value to the business community.

The charm of the area provides a pleasant atmosphere for both employees and the general public.

The use of gracious, historic buildings by the business community contributes to the professionalism and stability of business.

Obviously, having located our offices in a historic Haddonfield building, we are in favor of a historic district. However, careful consideration should be given to zoning procedures so as not to discourage the business community from restoring and preserving historic sites.

A. H. Williams & Co.
Alfred H. Williams, President

Don't

Forget

To

Vote

THE PROPOSED HISTORIC DISTRICT ORDINANCE HAS THE ENTHUSIASTIC SUPPORT OF THE HADDON FORTNIGHTLY AND THE HADDONFIELD HISTORICAL SOCIETY

(excerpts from a statement read by Mrs. Charles F. Wiggins, Jr., President of the Haddon Fortnightly, at the June 7 public hearing by the Planning Board)

"The Haddon Fortnightly is vitally interested in the proposed historic district zoning.

"We spend $14,000 of our budget to maintain one of the beautiful historic buildings for Haddonfield, and $2,770 goes to the borough in taxes.

"We have a continuing national program for community improvement. Seventeen members of our Community Improvement Committee surveyed the need of Haddonfield this year, and polled our club members as to our 1971-72 project. We elected to work for the rejuvenation of the business area, and the related goal of establishing an historic district.

"We asked that you begin immediately to implement the historic district zoning. We congratulate you for your efficient and prompt action in bringing the resolution to the public."

(excerpts from a letter sent to the Commissioners by Louis H. Goettelmann, president of the Haddonfield Historical Society and Elinor J. Jennings, Corresponding Secretary. This letter was sent after the entire society was polled as to whether or not they favored the enactment of an Historic District Ordinance. The result of the poll was overwhelming approval.)

"At the Annual Meeting the motion was made and unanimously passed that the Commissioners of the Borough of Haddonfield be earnestly requested to thoughtfully steer their concentration toward that intrinsic, potential value an Historic Preservation Ordinance would create.

"A large return of the ballots from the Historical Society Bulletin have all been cast in the affirmative.

"The Historical Society feels strongly that you will search every aspect that the ordinance shall make possible, and in so doing, realize as so many areas in our country have profitably learned, that such an enforcement can bring not only inherent charm to be enhanced, but accrued values in diversified facets that shall widely enrich our citizens and posterity."

WHO SAYS HISTORIC DISTRICT ZONING IS LEGAL?

THE STATE OF N. J. SAYS SO

The following information from the Chief of Historic Sites, Department of Environmental Protection, citing the opinion of the Chief Counsel for the Department was sent to the Solicitor of the Haddonfield Planning Board and a copy was subsequently sent to the Solicitor of the Borough. "The enabling legislation for creating an historic district zone is based on the Municipal Planning Act of 1953, Chapter 433, as revised in Chapter 287, Laws of 1966, to include historic sites. The important section for your purposes is 'the location and extent of scenic and historic sites'. In other words, a municipality may include a district as an historic site."

THREE N.J. TOWNS, 212 HISTORIC DISTRICTS SAY SO

State legislatures are not in the habit of passing unconstitutional legislation. State enabling legislation for Historic Districts has been upheld in the States where challenged. It has never been challenged nor struck down in any court in New Jersey.

THE U.S. SUPREME COURT SAYS SO

The court ruled in an unanimous decision: "The concept of public welfare is broad and inclusive...the values it represents are spiritual as well as physical, aesthetic as well as monetary...It is within the power of the legislature to determine that the community should be beautiful as well as healthy, spacious as well as clean...there is nothing in the Fifth Amendment (on individual property rights) to stand in the way."

THE CONGRESS OF THE U.S. SAYS SO

In 1966, the 89th Congress passed an Act "to establish a program for the preservation of additional historic properties throughout the Nation..." and authorized a national register of DISTRICTS, sites, buildings, structures and objects significant in American history, architecture, archeology, and culture..." It termed "historic preservation" to include the protection, rehabilitation, restoration and reconstruction of DISTRICTS, sites, buildings, etc.

"We have failed to realize that our architectural heritage is our biggest asset from both a residential and commercial point of view."

Ronald E. Shaffer, 8 Roberts Ave.
(owner of the historic Daniel Fortiner House, 1820)

RESTORATIONS OF HISTORIC HOUSES ACCORDING TO ARCHITECTURAL GUIDELINES greatly increase property values. (from left to right) Nathan Willits House, 1836, was restored by the late Herbert R. Leicht, architect. Daniel Fortiner House, 1820. Front windows were restored to original design by present owners, enhancing authenticity and beauty of entire facade. One of original Kay houses, 1790, 483 Kings highway east, restored by owners, was a "wreck," a town eyesore, is now one of our most beautiful and desirable historic houses. William Githens house and shop, 19-21 Potter street, would have been demolished for commercial use. Beautifully restored they were high income producing apartments, now a private home of a doctor. Its market value because of its historic beauty has steadily increased. THE HISTORIC DISTRICT ORDINANCE WOULD INSURE THAT FUTURE OWNERS WOULD NOT DEMOLISH OR DEFACE THESE HOUSES WITH TASTELESS ALTERATIONS AS HAS BEEN DONE IN DOZENS OF OTHER HISTORIC HOUSES HERE.

THIS IS WHAT CAN HAPPEN when you do not safeguard a DISTRICT instead of a few unconnected houses. The charming historic house on the left is at 34 Potter street. It was built about 1810 and knowledgeably restored by its present owners. It is blighted by the incompatible and ugly structure next to it. Indeed this structure blights one of our most picturesque historic streets in Haddonfield. Under the proposed Historic District Ordinance this violation of architectural harmony could not happen.

WHY A HISTORIC DISTRICT?

A walking tour of the Historic District of Haddonfield should convince you that it is vitally important to have an harmonious environment to protect and enhance our historic and architecturally significant homes and buildings.

On this page is but one example of many throughout the town. The historic Walt Whitman house in Camden is another. The deterioration of the area around that house and what it has done to the house itself violate our sense of history and aesthetics.

████████████████████████████████████
████████████████████████████████████
████████████████████████████████████
restored by a well-loved Historic District. Townspeople should preserve and enhance our own Society Hill in Philadelphia.

The sad experience has been that historic homes do not survive unless their environment survives. The pressures are too great to give them up for more downgraded uses, which adds to the total deterioration.

Thirdly, the business community profits immensely by the promotion of an "Historic District," as has already been demonstrated by the colonialization of our business district. One need only read the testimony from Annapolis, Md., on page 2 of this Supplement to realize what historic area planning can do to revive our retail shops which serve this residential town.

AN EXCELLENT EXAMPLE of how preservation of architectural authenticity beautifies and tasteless alteration "uglifies." Note the front windows. Mr. Wallace Root, 10 Tanner street, has zealously preserved the original facade of his building. The same structure next door was altered by previous owners to a commercial type "picture window." The present owners, antique dealers, would like to restore the original window treatment.

THE HENDRY-PENNYPACKER HOUSE, 255 Kings highway east, 1834. This house has both historic and architecturally significance. It was built by Dr. Charles Hendry, son of the prominent early citizen of Haddonfield, Dr. Bowman Hendry. Its architectural details such as this beautiful doorway are among the finest in South Jersey. The Historic District Ordinance would preserve these treasures no matter who the future owners.

CAN THIS BEAUTIFUL 18th CENTURY HOUSE ON HADDON AVE. SURVIVE?

(the historic 1793 John Estaugh Hopkins House, 65 Haddon avenue)
Surrounded by high density office buildings, parking lots, traffic congestion, more and more noise and pollution, will future owners be able to keep it as a residence?

ONLY THIS HISTORIC DISTRICT ORDINANCE CAN SAVE HADDONFIELD FROM URBAN SPRAWL AND DETERIORATION OF OUR QUALITY OF LIFE HERE

SECTION 1. Uses Permitted: All uses permitted in the Historic District shall be those designated by the Official Zoning Map. Such uses shall not be altered by further designation as an Historic District.

SECTION 2. Area and Height Regulations: Maximum building height, minimum lot size, maximum coverage, etc., shall be as provided in the Zoning Ordinance for the respective zones, except the Zoning Board of Adjustment may waive such regulations where necessary to preserve historic characteristics.

SECTION 3. Historic District Provisions: The following regulations shall apply in The Historic District and to those historic structures so designated outside the district and shall be in addition to the use districts or districts which shall also be designated by the Official Zoning Map and Articles of the Zoning Ordinance for such areas.

SECTION 4. Purpose: The purpose of this act is (1) to safeguard the heritage of the Borough of Haddonfield by preserving that part of the Borough which reflects elements of its cultural, social, economic and

There is absolutely no restriction on the color you paint your house

architectural history; (2) to maintain and develop an appropriate and harmonious setting for the historic and architecturally significant buildings, structures and places within that part of Haddonfield; (3) to stabilize and improve property values; (4) to foster civic beauty; (5) to promote the use of the historic district for the education, pleasure and welfare of the citizens of the Borough and its visitors.

SECTION 5. There is hereby established in the Borough of Haddonfield a district to be known as The Haddonfield Historic District. The bounds of The Haddonfield Historic District are defined for the purpose of this act as follows:

(Both sides of street are included unless otherwise designated)

1. Kings highway from the borough line on the east to Chews Landing road and Avondale avenue on the west.
2. Tanner street from Kings highway to Euclid avenue; Haddon avenue from Kings highway to and including No. 65 Haddon avenue.
3. Lake street from Haddon avenue to Grove street.
4. Grove street from Lake street to Kings highway on the west, and from Glover avenue to Kings highway on the east.
5. Warwick road from Kings highway to west Summit avenue.
6. Washington avenue from Kings highway to Cottage avenue.
7. Chestnut street from Kings highway to east Park avenue.
8. Centre street from Ellis street to east Park avenue.

You need not make any alterations, changes, or improvements for the entire life of your property, if you so wish

9. Potter street from Kings highway to Fowler avenue.
10. Clement street from Mechanic street to Tanner street.
11. Colonial avenue from Kings highway east to Lake street.
12. Friends avenue from Kings highway to Lake street.
13. Mechanic street from Kings highway east to Clement street.
14. Lincoln avenue from east Atlantic avenue to Centre street.
15. West Park avenue from Washington avenue to Warwick road.
16. East Park avenue from east Atlantic avenue to Centre street.
17. All of Westcoatt walk.
18. East Atlantic avenue from Lincoln avenue to east Park avenue.
19. West Cottage avenue (North side) from Washington avenue to Warwick road.
20. The following specific

Architectural guidelines need not add to costs... but do enhance and increase your property value

historic structures outside the physical boundaries of the Historic District, but which shall be considered part of the District:

a. William Estaugh Hopkins House, "Birdwood," on Hopkins lane (1794)

b. Birdwood Farmers Cottage, 405 Birdwood avenue (1796)

c. Samuel Wood House, 201 Wood lane (1844)

d. Elizabeth Haddon's Brew House, 201 Wood lane (1713)

e. Original Gill Country House, 80 Lane of Acres (1748)

f. Redman House, 140 Westment avenue (1834)

g. Campbell House, 540 Coles Mill road

h. Needles House, 392 Coles Mill road

i. 8 Roberts avenue (1820)

j. 22 Roberts avenue (1836)

k. J. Gill House, 613 Warwick road (1853)

The boundary lines of The Haddonfield Historic District, as generally defined by the several streets, shall be the existing rear boundary lot line, as of the date of

Administration of ordinance is as simple as in present zoning ordinance

this act, of the lots bordering on the outside lines of the streets named as boundaries, or two hundred feet from the outside line of the streets named as boundaries, whichever is the lesser distance.

SECTION 6. Duties and Powers. (1) It shall be the duty of the Building Inspector to review all plans for construction, alteration, repair, moving or demolition of structures in the historic district and to submit those applications to the Planning Board which involve changes in existing exterior architectural features or new construction involving architectural features. The Planning Board shall then, pursuant to N.J.S.A. 40:55-1. 13, make its recommendation to the Building Inspector as to approval or disapproval of the plans under this ordinance withir thirty (30) days. If the Planning Board disapproves the plans under this section, the Building Inspector shall deny the application and the applicant may proceed before the Zoning Board of Adjustment.

(2) No building or structure shall hereafter be erected, reconstructed, altered, restored or demolished within The Haddonfield Historic District unless and until an application for a building permit shall have been approved as to exterior architectural features which are subject to public view from a public street, way, or place. Evidence of such required approval shall be a Certificate of Approval issued by the Planning Board.

(3) In reviewing the plans, the Planning Board shall give consideration to:

a. the historical or architectural value and significance of the structure and its relationship to the historic value of the surrounding area;

b. the general compatibility of exterior design, arrangement and materials proposed to be used; and

c. any other factor, including aesthetic, which it deems pertinent;

d. the attached description of the details of design for the period of architecture involved in the particular structure and surrounding neighborhood;

e. the attached plat indicating the areas in which the various architectural styles preponderate in the District.

The Planning Board shall pass only on exterior features of a structure and shall not consider interior arrangements, nor shall it disapprove applications except in regard to considerations as set forth in the previous paragraph.

It is the intent of this Section that the Planning Board be strict in its judgment of plans for alteration, repair or demolition of existing structures deemed to be valuable according to studies, approved by the Planning Board of the Borough of Haddonfield, by qualified persons using as the Criteria of Evaluation those developed by the National Trust for Historic Preservation. A list of such structures designated by street address is appended by guide the Planning Board in its judgments.

It is the intent of this Section that the Planning Board shall encourage any alterations or repairs to structures on this list be made in the spirit of their architectural style, and that any additions will be made in such a manner as not to detract from a building's original appearance.

The buildings included on the list are those structures within the district that are deemed to be valuable for the period of architecture they represent and important to the neighborhood within which they exist. It is intended that demolition of these structures should be discouraged as their loss will be a common loss to the Borough and the neighborhood. Moving of a structure on the list should be encouraged as an alternative to demolition, if there is no other way to save the structure.

This ordinance does not change existing zoning uses

WHAT'S AN HISTORIC HOUSE?

The quality of significance in American history, architecture, archeology and culture is present in districts, sites, buildings, structures and objects of state and location importance that possess integrity of location, design, setting, materials, workmanship, feeling and association, and:

1. that are associated with events that have made a significant contribution to the broad patterns of our history; or
2. that are associated with the lives of persons significant in our past; or
3. that embody the distinctive characteristics of a type, period, or method of construction, or that represent the work of a master, or that posses high artistic values, or that represent a significant and distinguishable entity whose components may lack individual distinction; or
4. that have yielded, or may be likely to yield, information important in pre-history or history.
5. that best exemplify the broad cultural, political, economic or social history of the nation, state or community and from which the visitor may grasp in three-dimensional form one of the larger patterns of the American heritage.

It is also the intent of this Section that the Planning Board shall be lenient in its judgment of plans for new construction or for alterations, repair, or demolition of structures of little historic value not shown on the list which are within The Haddonfield Historic District, except where such construction, alteration, repair or demolition would seriously impair the historic value and character of surrounding structures or the surrounding area.

Demolition or removal may be forbidden or postponed for a period of six months (after public hearing granted to applicant if desired) and the Planning Board shall then consult civics groups and public agencies to ascertain how the Borough may preserve the building and/or premises. The Planning Board is empowered to work out with the owner feasible plans for preservation of structures where moving or demolition thereof would be a great loss to the public and to the Borough.

When it is necessary to move an historic building to another site within the Borough to preserve it, upon approval of the relocations plans by the Planning Board, said building may be relocated providing it fulfills the area regulations of said zone as to lot size, set back, and yard area.

The Planning Board shall have the power to engage experts to aid in its deliberations. The Planning Board shall have the power to issue a Certificate of Approval, if it approves of the plans submitted to it for its review. A building permit shall not be issued until such Certificate of Approval has been issued by the Planning Board.

The Planning Board, in passing appropriateness of exterior architectural features, in any case, shall keep in mind the purposes set forth in Section 4, and shall consider among other things the general design, arrangements, and material of the building or structure in question and the relationship of such factors to similar features of historic structures in the immediate surroundings, and the position of such structures in relationship to the street or public way.

The Planning Board shall not consider features not subject to public view. The Planning Board shall not make any recommendations or requirements except for the purpose of preventing developments obviously incongruous to the historic aspects of the surroundings and The Haddonfield Historic District.

In case of disapproval, the Planning Board shall state its reasons therefore in writing and it may make recommendations to the applicant with respect to appropriateness of design, arrangement, material and the like, of the structure involved.

Upon approval of the plans, the Planning Board shall cause a Certificate of Approval, dated and signed by the chairman, to be issued to the applicant or affixed to the plans.

If the Planning Board shall fail to take action in any case within thirty (30) days after receipt of any application for a certificate of approval or a permit for removal, the case shall be deemed to be approved except where mutual agreement has been reached for an extension of the time limit.

SECTION 7. Nothing in this ordinance shall prohibit repairing or rebuilding any structure in The District so as to maintain or return the structure to its original condition prior to deterioration or destruction.

SECTION 8. On applications for a variance following the refusal of the Planning Board to issue a Certificate of Approval, the Zoning Board shall be controlled by the standards set forth in this ordinance in considering the merits of the application.

SECTION 9. The Planning Board shall appoint a five-member advisory committee composed of residents with experience and/or educational qualifications pertinent to preservation of historic structures. This committee shall be available for consultation with the Planning Board and the Zoning Board to aid in deliberations on applications under this section. Members of this advisory committee shall be representative of the community, including The Haddonfield Historic District.

SECTION 10. The procedure for application for variance before the Zoning Board of Adjustment shall be the same as the procedure utilized to obtain a variance pursuant to the existing rules and regulations of the Zoning Board of Adjustment.

SECTION 11. Appeals may be taken to the Borough Board of Commissioners by any person aggrieved by a ruling of the Zoning Board. The Borough Board of Commissioners shall hear and act upon such appeals promptly and the decision of the Board shall be as determined by a majority vote of the members of the Board of Commissioners.

"The day of the retail merchant in Haddonfield is over. Haddonfield will be the next office center of Camden County."

The Preservation Society contended that the promotion of the Historic District of which the business district on King's Highway was a part, would improve the aesthetics of the district and make the historic identity of the district a shopper attraction. The Preservation Society's view proved the right one because the Historic District Ordinance did indeed become a major factor in the rejuvenation of the business community.

There were those who proclaimed in print that Haddonfield should forget its past and "supposedly glorious history and heritage." But the Preservation Society embarked on a strong campaign to win the referendum and save the town's glorious history and heritage.

In the October 28, 1971 issue of the *Haddon Gazette*, the last edition before the November 2 referendum, there appeared a "blitz" of articles and advertisements on both sides. The opposition article and advertisements were anonymous.

The Preservation Society published a four-page Supplement with ten photographs illustrating the assets of the proposed Historic District, and answering the opposing arguments with hard facts. The back page of the Supplement reprinted the entire Historic District Ordinance with large boldface type answering the most common fears about the Ordinance. On the inside page were headlines proclaiming the potential benefits of the Ordinance:

ANNAPOLIS MAYOR CREDITS HISTORIC PRESERVATION WITH 112 PERCENT INCREASE IN PROPERTY VALUES ... "GOOD FOR BUSINESS AND GOOD FOR THE COMMUNITY AS A WHOLE."

Another headline, backed up with facts:

THE HISTORIC DISTRICT ORDINANCE IS PROTECTIVE, NOT "RESTRICTIVE."

And to answer the Commissioners there appeared four authoritative sources to establish the legality of the Historic District Ordinance: the Chief Counsel for the N.J. Department of Environmental Protection; Historic Districts established elsewhere (212 at that time-now over 2000); The Congress of the United States; and the United States Supreme Court which ruled in a unanimous decision:

"The concept of public welfare is broad and inclusive... the values it represents are spiritual as well as physical, aesthetic as well as monetary...It is within the power of the legislature to determine that the community should be beautiful as well as healthy, spacious as well as clean...there is nothing in the Fifth Amendment (on individual property rights) to stand in the way."

THE REFERENDUM

November 2, 1971 – the referendum to create a Historic District Ordinance was approved by 62 percent of the vote in all ten voting districts. Once more the citizens of Haddonfield had elected to remain "A Pleasant Town."

In just a few years the success of the Historic District had become apparent. On the tenth anniversary of Historic District Zoning, William Taylor, former chairman of the Haddonfield Planning Board, stated:

"It is a very happy occasion that we celebrate the tenth anniversary of Historic District Zoning in the Borough of Haddonfield. The beneficial results of this zoning are evident throughout the Borough. The homes and buildings within the Historic District have been preserved and steadily improved to the extent that people are coming from around the country to see the success of the program. The business district has been greatly enhanced by the program which is made evident by the success of the new and previously existing specialty shops, banking establishments and other commercial and professional enterprises. All of the residential districts of Haddonfield have benefitted by upgrading the center of town. There can no longer be any doubt that Historic District Zoning has improved the Borough and we are indebted to those people who have made it possible."

The National Register

The Historic District Ordinance had halted the demolition of significant structures. Applications for alterations and additions were now capably reviewed by the Historic District Advisory Committee, established by the Ordinance. The first Committee members were Louis H. Goettelmann, chairman, Joan L. Aiken, John Wood, William Blake and Del Stephenson, to be replaced by Harry Atkinson when Stephenson resigned. But the Committee knew that the historic district was vulnerable to encroachment of, or destruction by, any state, county or municipally funded or initiated project. Therefore, in October, 1979, the Haddonfield Preservation Society applied for listing in the State and National Register of Historic Places, which gave a measure of protection to properties from such encroachment and destruction. Louis H. Goettelmann and Joan L. Aiken of the Society prepared the application which included an Inventory and Description of the 488 structures and sites in the District. The state approval in 1980 came none too soon as it halted the widening of Potter Street and Grove Street, two of the oldest streets in Haddonfield. It meant destroying almost 100 trees and making a freeway of the most picturesque historic street in the town. On July 21, 1982, Haddonfield was listed on the National Register of Historic Places; but the State listing in 1980 saved a section of the historic core of Haddonfield. It was wise to enact the Historic District Ordinance first, in 1971, to stop demolitions and unsightly alterations which the National Register listing could not do. However the listing did add another measure of protection to the Historic District and enabled qualified properties in the Historic District to obtain tax credits for restoration and rehabilitation.

Note: Members of the Planning Board who voted to approve the Historic District Ordinance and sent it to the Commissioners to act on it by August, 1971.

Richard A. Walter, Chairman; Ann B. Ward, Vice Chairman;
Robert J. Twitchell; George M. von Uffel;
Parker Griffeth; Russell Hunt; Helen C. Kulp;
Eugene V. Hinski, Mayor; C. Franklin Fretz, Commissioner;
Michael Patrick King, Esq. Solicitor

What others say…

REALTORS:

The preservation of historic buildings in the residential and commercial district has made Haddonfield the most desirable town in South Jersey for both business and residential homeowners. The strong real estate values that Haddonfield residents each share can be directly attributed to the preservation of the original architectural designs and historic colors of the commercial and residential buildings. With proper preservation, restoration and colors, most property owners will enjoy 15-25 percent increased value of their homes.

> Jack Leonard, Realtor
> Roney, Vermaat & Leonard

Historic District zoning has proved to be good economics. Ratables in the district have increased substantially, better than 60 percent. Historic District zoning gives prestige to the entire town, the residential and business area, not just the Historic District. The demand for old houses to restore increases every year.

> George Roney, Realtor
> Roney, Vermaat & Leonard

The whole tour was such a success! You have done so much for our preservation. There is no way that our town can thank you. Your gift of love, commitment and excellence is immeasurable.

> Mark Lenny, Realtor
> Fox & Lazo

HISTORIANS

Am so happy that you have had another well deserved award. Your "District" has not only aided Haddonfield— but has put Haddonfield again "on the map" for today and posterity.

> Beatrice Stuckert, former Director
> Haddonfield Public Library

There is not a person in Haddonfield who does not owe you a debt for insisting that the community retain a sense of its heritage through its historical architecture, instead of, as has happened in far too many years…let it go to pot and eventually destroy it. Haddonfield is a richer, more interesting town because its past, present and future are so harmoniously intermingled. It happened because of your persistence and perseverance.

> Patricia Lennon, member of Haddonfield Planning Board,
> former President, Historical Society

GOVERNMENT

Haddonfield does indeed have a great deal to be proud of for its efforts in historic preservation. But, as you said, preservation work is never done. Therefore, as you continue your efforts, please let us know if the Office of New Jersey Heritage can provide you assistance. I look forward to working with you again.

> Nancy L. Zerbe, Administrator
> Office of New Jersey Heritage

I salute the members of the Preservation Society for your leadership in urging the Haddonfield Commission to pass the Historic District Ordinance. By becoming the second municipality in New Jersey to enact this legislation, you have provided leadership to the state on the importance of preserving the heritage of our past for future generations.

> Bill Bradley, United States Senator

Mobilizing Public Opinion for Historic Preservation
Making it Work

by Joan L. Aiken

"Mobilizing Public Opinion," written by Joan L. Aiken was included in and is reprinted from *PRESERVING NEW JERSEY, A Handbook for Municipal Historic Preservation Commissions* (sponsored by Rutgers University and Preservation New Jersey).

There are three levels of historic preservation efforts. All three must be addressed if historic preservation is to succeed at the local level. The essential ingredient in the success of each level is a strong public education program.

The three levels are:

1. **Mobilizing public opinion to approve the enactment of a Historic District Ordinance.**

2. **Public acceptance of and cooperation with the administration of the Historic District Ordinance.**

3. **A continuing education program to promote awareness of and appreciation for the town's architectural heritage, to promote preservation, restoration, and rehabilitation, and to foster the knowledge of and civic pride in the architectural history of the community.**

MOBILIZING PUBLIC OPINION TO ENACT A LOCAL HISTORIC DISTRICT CODE

How to overcome obstacles and shape public attitudes:

It is important to identify your "Publics" and evaluate the self-interests, fears, and motivations of each. The interests of a community are not homogeneous. Nowhere is this truer than in the area of historic preservation. What appeals to property owners within a proposed district is quite different from the appeals that win favor outside the district where property owners feel they are not affected or restricted.

In Haddonfield, and in most communities, the "Publics" evaluated for their special interests in order to determine the effective appeals to change negative attitudes to positive ones are:

1. The Planning Board, which is empowered to develop and recommend new zoning ordinances and to develop a master plan.

2. The elected officials who have final approval of ordinances.

3. Property owners in the proposed historic district who fear restrictions on their property.

4. Property owners outside the district who cannot see any benefit for them in historic zoning. Their apathy is a chief obstacle.

5. The real estate fraternity - brokers, bankers, insurance and mortgage companies who claim historic zoning will restrict development.

6. The business/merchant community which fears design and sign provisions in the ordinance will increase costs of alterations.

7. The civic organizations, whose endorsement has considerable influence; there is opportunity to appeal to their self interest.

8. The education establishment.

PERSUASION IS COMMUNICATION:

In Haddonfield we drew up an appeal to each of our "Publics" based on the Principals of Persuasion and used every communication tool to reach these "Publics" with these appeals.

COMMUNICATION TOOLS

The Press: Making News. Getting it printed. The Press will report provocative programs and prominent speakers and will quote authorities.

Haddonfield's four-page supplement was inserted in the local paper and distributed to every household. *PRESERVING HISTORIC HADDONFIELD* had an electric effect on the entire community.

Success stories:

a series of articles on historic districts in other communities that have been an economic boon to those communities.

Letters to the Editor signed by influential people.

Carefully prepared statements at public meetings—planning board meetings, commission meetings—in the presence of reporters which will be reported in the press.

Editorial survey of public opinion on historic preservation.

Community Programs:

Programs open to all. Symposiums, noted speakers, topics that appeal to self interest: "The Dollars and Cents of Historic Preservation" (Talk by Frederick Haupt, Director of Information, National Trust).

Color Slide Lecture:

Presentation of the most distinguished historic houses in the district—an architectural tour. The narration is most important and is keyed to changing negative attitudes.

The Newsletter:

News of coming programs and speakers; column on "What's doing in the Historic District." Material on restorations, an insert page of technical assistance: historic roofs, synthetic siding, porches, steps, fences, repairs, etc.

The Awards Program

The High School Essay Program

Radio and Television Interviews

Frequency and repetition are fundamental to the success of good communication. The benefits and the positive aspects of historic preservation must be repeated in as many ways as possible and as frequently as possible. A creative approach will be helpful.

THE SUCCESSFUL ADMINISTRATION OF THE ORDINANCE

After the historic district ordinance is adopted, the crucial work of successful implementation begins. Some important things to remember are:

1. The public must understand the purpose and provisions of the ordinance and believe that the visible results will enhance individual and community property values, the beauty of the town, and the quality of the environment. In Haddonfield a letter was sent to every property owner in the district advising him of the benefits of the new ordinance and the procedures for applications for alterations, additions, repairs, replacements, etc.

2. The top-level qualifications of the Historic District Commission give authority to the decisions on applications.

3. Commission members work with the applicant on a one-to-one basis, often having the chairman visit the site and work out the changes so they meet the approved standards—stressing the benefits of "doing it right."

4. The Commission Report on each application not only gives a detailed analysis of the reasons for approval or denial, but in the latter case, give constructive alternatives to merit approval on resubmission. Also, each report "educates" the Planning Board which must be convinced of the merit of the Commission's recommendations (history of the structure, architectural merit, streetscape, etc. and reference to ordinance provision on which the decision was made.)

5. A continuing education program by the Haddonfield Preservation Society is a support system to the Historic District Commission, which cannot undertake the same community programs to promote historic preservation.

Continuing Education Program

A strong local preservation group can promote public understanding of the provisions of the ordinance and cooperation in its enforcement.

Education Programs:

Annual house tours in the Historic District tie in with National Historic Preservation Week in May. The theme of each tour promotes some important aspect of historic preservation. Examples: "Rewards of Restoration—Doing it Right," "The Care and Feeding of Historic Houses," "Painting the American Historic House," "Centennial Historic Houses," "Gardens in the Historic District," "Victorian Heyday in Haddonfield: Restored Houses of the Victorian Period."

Lectures

on preservation subjects by excellent speakers.

Conferences: A New Look at The Indian King (Historic Site)

Christmas at the Indian King (to promote attendance at our most important historic site).

Principles of Persuasion

1. FEAR

The appeal to a person's fears is one of the most potent motivations for changing attitudes. Examples: Fear of urban sprawl, fear of overdevelopment, fear of creeping commercialism, fear of being engulfed by high rise, high density buildings; fear of the proliferation of parking lots destroying valuable green space; fear of utility and government encroachment, etc. Each municipality has its special threats and pressures which the community perceives will downgrade the environment and decrease property values.

Dramatize these threats. Emphasize them graphically.

2. SELF-INTEREST

People act to satisfy their own needs and desires, not those of the governing body, the official boards, or preservation groups. What are these needs and desires? Appeal must stress personal benefits to the property owner or group you are trying to persuade.

You can influence a person's attitudes and behavior only by creating inner sources of satisfactions.

People are perverse. They have their own ideas of what they want and stubbornly refuse to be moved by appeals to motives which other people think they have or should have.

Before trying to change someone's mind, find out what motivates it and focus on the real motives.

3. MOTIVES

a. The economic motive—Research and present all the facts proving there is more economic satisfaction for supporting historic preservation than not supporting it.

b. Desire for status-prestige—An important influence on people's attitudes towards their community. Historic preservation gives the community, the District, distinction. Fosters civic pride. Exploit this motive. A realtor in Haddonfield gave us this testimonial: "Historic District Zoning gives prestige to the entire town, the residential and business area, not just the Historic District. The demand for old houses to restore increases every year."

c. Rewards and Punishments—Both rewards and punishments motivate attitudes and behavior but they have different effects. We can get someone to do what we want by rewarding him. Never cease to emphasize the rewards of historic preservation, never allude to the "punishments."

Example: Never use punishment words like "restrictions," "controls," "regulations." Instead, Historic District Zoning rewards you with "protection" of your property value, protection of your streetscape, protection of your neighborhood. Rewards you with free architectural counsel when and if you want to make alterations, additions, repairs, replacements, etc. Rewards you, above all, with a substantial increase in the market value of your property. Rewards the town with increased tax ratables.

Cite examples: Society Hill, Philadelphia; Cape May, New Jersey; Burlington, Bridgeton, Haddonfield and dozens of other towns. Obtain the statistical figures for proof.

4. WHO SAYS IT?

What you say is not only important, but who says it.
People will listen to recognized authorities in the
field, people who have first-hand experience with
historic district zoning, such as Mayors of towns which
have these ordinances. They may say the same thing
you are saying, but their authority has the clout.

Examples of "authorities" who spoke in Haddonfield
on subjects which persuasively overcame some of the
negative arguments:

Frederick Haupt
Director of Information, National Trust, "The Dollars
and Cents of Historic Preservation"

Gilbert Crandall
Chief of Tourist Division, Annapolis, Md., "Economic
Value of Historic Preservation"

Richard W. Huffman
Director, Area Planning and Urban Design,
Philadelphia City Planning Commission. "The
Economics of Historic Preservation" - "Planner Says
Historic Areas Sky-Rocket Land Values."

Bruce Minnix
Mayor of Cape May

Carolyn Pitts
Professional preservationist, did the survey of every
building in the Historic District of Cape May

David Poinsett
Former Supervisor of Historic Sites (Administrator,
Historic Preservation Section, Dept. Environmental
Protection) "Why a Historic District?" (To refute those
who would preserve only a few historic houses, but
not a District).

Maps

THOMAS SHARP MAP, 1700

The original of Thomas Sharp's 1700 map of Newton Township, Gloucester County, New Jersey, is in the manuscript collection of John Clement's papers in the Pennsylvania Historical Society Library, Philadelphia. Three symbols for buildings in Haddonfield were drawn on this map by Sharp:

1. *On the tract bought from Willis by John Haddon the building near Cooper's Creek. This by tradition is believed to have been Elizabeth Haddon's first residence in 1701 when she first landed in Newton Township. It also shows on the sketch made in 1686 by Sharp of his first survey of the Willis holdings.*
2. *On the tract belonging to Joseph Collins, the house built by his father Francis Collins, the first house to be built by a white settler in 1682, when he settled in what is now Haddonfield.*
3. *The "Smith's shop" located near the head of the stream which now feeds Hopkins Pond. This is the Mathews tract bought by John Haddon about 1699, and is believed to have been built by a blacksmith sent here from England by Mathews to start building up the local economy as an aid to developing the land.*

HISTORIC DISTRICT ZONE

King's Highway was laid out in 1681 over a portion of the trail of the Lenni Lenape Indians, running from Perth Amboy to Salem. The Highway was constructed 100 feet wide for the King of England to visit his colony with his entourage.

Haddonfield in 1686, when the "Salem Road" was completed, was a one-street town and development was along the road, then down the side streets as they were cut through for the growing village. The boundary of the Historic District was drawn to encompass this historic core of the town.

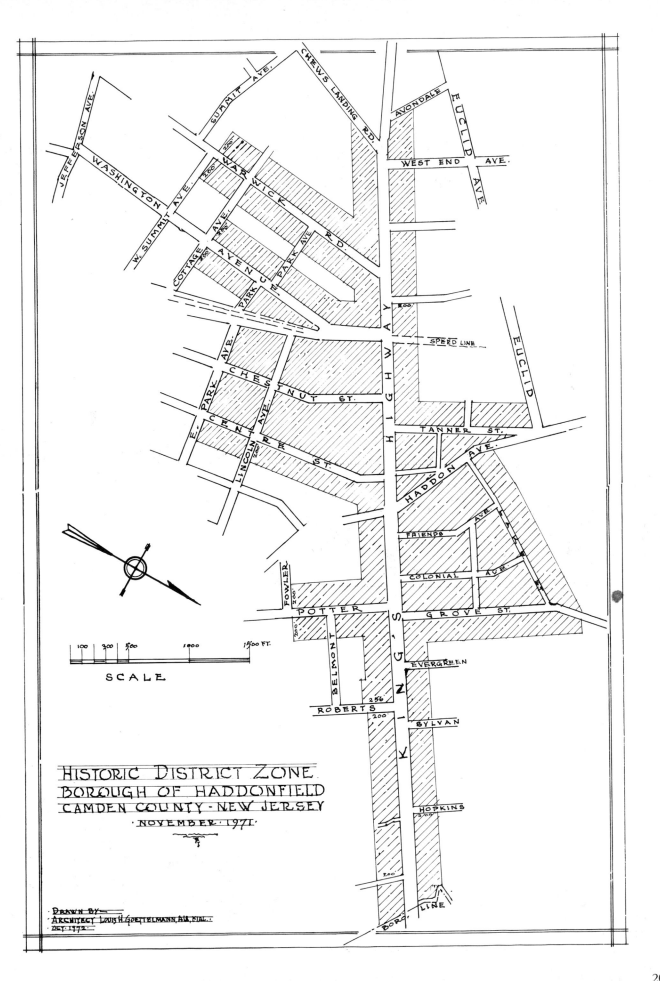

SCALE

HISTORIC DISTRICT ZONE
BOROUGH OF HADDONFIELD
CAMDEN COUNTY · NEW JERSEY
· NOVEMBER · 1971 ·

Drawn By
Architect Louis H. Goettelmann A.I.A., P.I.A.L.
Oct. 1972

Glossary

We are grateful to Dr. Roger Moss,
author of *Victorian Exterior Decoration,*
for permission to reprint the
excellent glossary in that book.

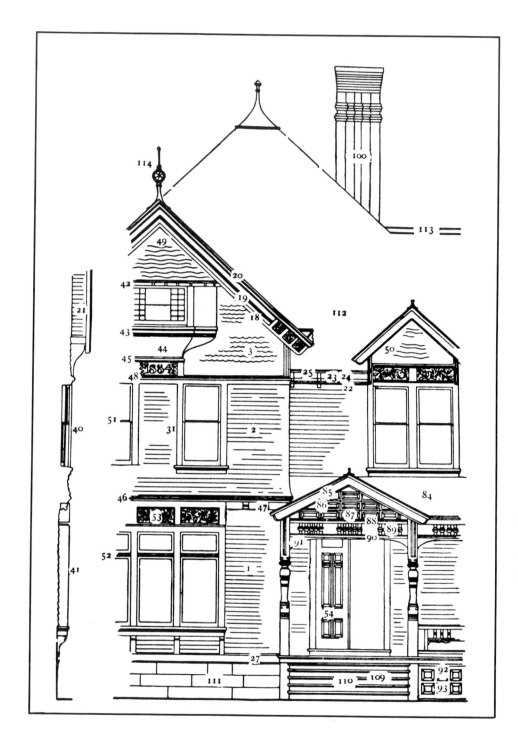

1.–3. **Body**
    1. First story
    2. Second story
    3. Attic
4.–25. **Cornice**
    4. Edge of crown mold
    5. Crown
    6. Fascia
    7. Bed mold
    8. Dentals
    9. Frieze
    10. Panel mold
    11. Panel
    12. Architrave
    13. Sunken face of sandwich bracket
    14. Raised face of sandwich bracket
    15. Bracket panel
    16. Bracket margin
    17. Soffit
    18.–20. Bargeboard
    21. Ceiling under eaves
    22. Foot pieces
    23. Gutter face
    24. Gutter brackets
    25. Gutter cap
26. **Corner Board**
27.–30. **Water Table**
    28. Slope
    29. Edge
    30. Face
31.–45. **Window Frame or Casing**
    32. Face
    33. Cap fillet
    34. Cap mold
    35. Cap panel
    36. Keystone
    37. Chamfer
    38. Sill

39. Apron
40. Reveal
41. Edge
42. Attic window cornice
43. Attic window sill mold
44. Attic window cove
45. Attic window base mold
46. **Belt Course**
47. **Beam Ends**
48. **Attic Belt Course**
49.–50. **Tympanum**
51. **Window Sash**
52. **Window Transom**
53. **Cut Work**
54.–57. **Doors**
    54. Stiles and rails
    55. Mold
    56. Receding part of panel
    57. Projecting part of panel
58.–59. **Shutters (Blinds)**
    58. Louvers (slats)
    59. Frame
60.–93. **Porch**
    60. Balustrade post
    61. Balustrade base
    62. Balustrade rail
    63. Receding part of baluster
    64. Projecting part of baluster
    65. Abacus
    66. Capital
    67. Neck mold
    68. Chamfer
    69. Shaft
    70. Rosette
    71. Plinth
    72. Plinth mold
    73. Rail
    74. Dado
    75. Dado panel
    76. Base

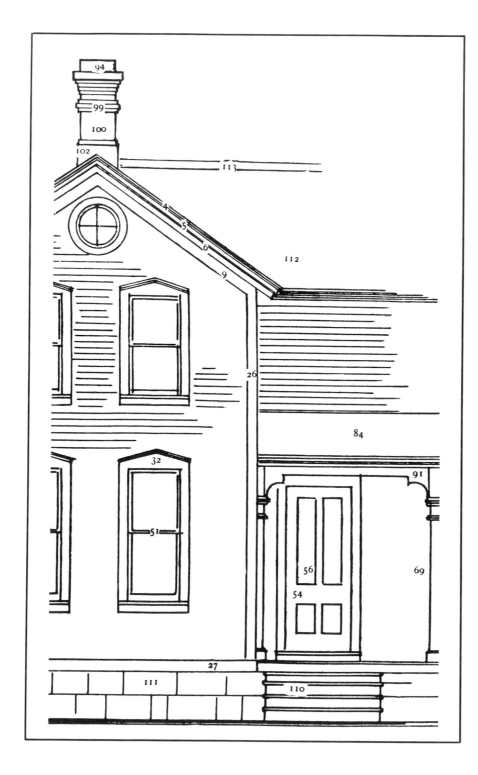

77. Base mold
78. Ornamental rail
79. Ornamental panel
80. Ornamental chamfer
81. Bead below steps
82. Panel mold below steps
83. Panel below steps
84. Roof
85. Face rafter (bargeboard)
86. Gable rail
87. Gable panels
88. Plate
89. Cornice balusters
90. Cornice rail
91. Cornice bracket
92. Rails below
93. Panels below

94.–102. Chimney
94. Top of cap
95. Crown mold of cap
96. Fascia of cap
97. Bed mold of cap
98. Frieze of cap
99. Architrave
100. Shaft
101. Panels
102. Base

103.–108. Fence
103. Post
104. Post chamfer
105. Upper rail
106. Lower rail
107. Base
108. Pickets (balusters)

109.–110. Steps
109. Tread mold
110. Riser

111. Foundation

112.–114. Roof
113. Ridge roll or cresting
114. Iron finials (also common location for acroterion)

Bibliography

History of Camden County, New Jersey, George R. Prowell,
L.J. Richards & Co., (Philadelphia) 1886

Some Noteworthy Homes in Haddonfield, Elizabeth Hopkins Lenhart,
Haddonfield Preservation Society, 1974

Inventory and Description Houses, Building & Sites
The Historic District of Haddonfield, Louis H. Goettelmann, Joan L. Aiken,
Haddonfield Preservation Society

300th Anniversary Settlement of Haddonfield,
(Souvenir Program); Joan L. Aiken, Editor,
Haddonfield Preservation Society, 1982

History of the First Baptist Church of Haddonfield, NJ,
Sarah Crawford Hillman

This is Haddonfield,
Historical Society of Haddonfield, N.J. 1963

Verse and Prose of James Lane Pennypacker
Historical Society of Haddonfield, NJ 1936

Insurance Records, John Lewis Rowand, Book 1-3,
Historical Society of Haddonfield, NJ

Sloan's Victorian Buildings, Samuel Sloan,
Dover Publications, New York, 1980

The American Heritage History of Notable American Homes,
American Heritage Publishing Company, 1971

Treasury of Early American Homes, Richard Pratt,
Curtis Publishing Company, 1946

Descriptions of Haddonfield Historic Homes, Newsletters,
Preserving Historic Haddonfield,
Haddonfield Preservation Society, 1973-1991